The Coldest Night

Rob Gering

Disclaimer

This book is a memoir based on true events. It reflects the author's present recollections of experiences over time. Some names and characteristics have been changed, some events have been compressed, and some dialogue has been recreated.

Dedication

This book could not have been written without someone stopping that very cold morning to investigate one glove lying on the side of the trail. I'd like to dedicate this book to Ron, for being that person, and also his riding group, for playing a huge role in my rescue.

Acknowledgment

I would like to thank my incredible partner, Sue, for helping me navigate this difficult task of telling my story. She was by my side through every paragraph.

To my kids, Nicholas and Madison, for being the awesome people they are. I am so proud of you both, and I cannot wait to be a part of your next chapters.

My family and close friends were there for me then and still are today. I look forward to making many more memories with you.

About the Author

Rob Gering is a retired career firefighter who lives with his girlfriend, Sue, in the beautiful Northwoods of Wisconsin. Rob is an Air Force veteran and a Fox Valley Tech College graduate in Fire Protection. He is a father of two awesome and loving children who, to this day, are pursuing their dreams across this great American country.

Preface

During my career as a firefighter, I've encountered many different types of emergencies. I am trained to assess critical situations and to recognize potential solutions. I never, in my lifetime, thought I would be on the other side of one of those situations. My story starts with a fun-filled day of snowmobiling with friends in northern Wisconsin. After leaving my friends that night and traveling back to my cabin alone, something happened that would change my life in ways I would never have imagined. I spent the coldest night of my life alone in the woods, severely injured unable to move. The agony of the pain, and the torment my mind put me through is just the beginning of my story.

Contents

Chapter 1: The Night of the Accident

In the heart of a serene, snow-draped forest in northern Wisconsin, the night air was charged with an expectant silence as if the trees held their breath. Beneath the watchful gaze of a billion stars, the only sound to reach my ears was the distant howl of a lone Coyote, its cry echoing through the vast, untouched wilderness.

The weather was unforgiving. The temperature had plummeted to several degrees below zero, the cold that seeps into your bones and reminds every breath of winter's dominion over the land.

The snow underfoot was fresh, a powdery layer that covered the ground like a blanket, undisturbed except for the trail left by my Artic Cat 660 snowmobile. The moon, a hint of silver in the sky, cast a pale light over the landscape, giving the snow an ethereal glow.

The cold bit deep - a fierce reminder of winter's grip, as the fresh snow lay untouched, transforming the landscape into a scene of a beautiful picture I once saw.

The morning, February 23rd, broke clear and bright, the sun casting its warmth against the chill of the dawn. With anticipation for the day's adventure, I stepped out from my cabin into the brilliant sunlight, ready to join my friends on the snowmobile trails.

Dressed in my riding gear—bibs, jacket, gloves, and boots, all of which were made by the Yamaha corporation (got a deal on them) —I was a figure prepared for the day's challenges. The outfit, designed specifically for snowmobiling, combined function with style: the jacket and bibs, a striking black with white lettering, protected against the cold and made a bold statement against the white snow. The gloves and boots, essential for warmth and control, completed my armor against the winter elements and were perfect for the adventure that I had planned today.

Our love for the thrill of the ride drew us together, a band of friends speeding over the snow, weaving through the forests and across frozen lakes. It was our ritual to embrace the frosty winter, finding joy in the rush of the cold air and the freedom of the open trail.

As the day unfolded, our group grew, picking up another friend at a gas station and yet another further north. We became a convoy of laughter and stories, our engines humming a tune of camaraderie and adventure. The landscape blurred into a rush of white and blue, the sun overhead guiding us through the trails.

We were snowmobiling and making the most of the last day at my cabin, as after that, I had to return to Green Bay, and the days off were going to be over.

When the sun began its descent, marking the end of our journey, a sense of contentment settled over me. The day had been great with the bonds of friendship and the sheer exhilaration of snowmobiling.

As we parted ways, I carried with me the memories of a perfect day, a reminder of the simple joys that make life so rich and how our ritual was still going. I was thinking of the chores that awaited me at the cabin, and my dog Kelso was probably curled up on the couch, wondering where I was.

Saying goodbye to my friends, I turned my snowmobile south and left alone. The trail was familiar, almost like a friend guiding me home because I had been doing that for the previous two days, but as the darkness covered the surroundings more, a sense of anticipation grew inside me.

Something about the quiet of the approaching night, the way the cold seemed to sharpen my thoughts, made me feel like I was on the edge of a significant moment. The journey back felt different as if it was marking the end of the day and the beginning of a story. A story that was mine to live and later to tell. I thought this was just goodbye and continued my journey, lost in the day's thoughts.

As the darkness began to cover even the slightest of light, my heart was full from the day's adventures. Alone now, I revved my snowmobile, the familiar hum beneath me a comforting presence as I set off back to my cabin. The trail, a ribbon through the wilderness, was a path I had traveled many times, each bend and straight as familiar as the back of my hand.

The tranquility of the ride throughout the day and the beauty of the surrounding forest bathed in the setting sun's soft light were a stark contrast to the adrenaline-fueled hours that had now begun. Lost in my thoughts, replaying the day's events and the laughter shared, I was unaware of the moment that would shatter the peace and alter the course of my night.

Without warning, a deer—camouflaged against the winter landscape, its coat blending seamlessly with the brush—darted out from nowhere. In an instant, I found myself brushing up against it. Either my sled hit the deer, or the deer hit my body, the impact throwing me out of control. There was no time to react, no opportunity to swerve or brake, only the sudden, terrifying realization that I was headed straight toward a curve and off the trail.

My body hit a series of trees, each impact a brutal punctuation in the moment's chaos. The world spun, a dizzying blur of snow, sky, and forest until I landed face down in the snow with a heavy thud.

The silence that followed was complete. The forest around me suddenly still, as if holding its breath.

Pain crashed over me in waves, a sharp, all-consuming agony that anchored me to the reality of my situation. I was lying on top of my badly broken arms, the weight of my body pressing down, intensifying the pain.

My left leg was an abstract of torment, severely broken and ensnared in a branch close to the ground, twisting it at an unnatural angle. The cold seeped into my bones, and the snow beneath me was a cold bed that offered no comfort.

In all pitch darkness, alone and injured, the reality of my situation began to dawn on me. I was trapped, unable to move. My snowmobile, a silent witness to the accident, came to rest just a few feet away. The forest, so beautiful and serene just moments before, now felt vast and indifferent, a wilderness untroubled by the plight of a lone snowmobiler.

The pain, the cold, the realization of my vulnerability—it all merged into a single, overwhelming panic. Yet, as the initial shock began to subside, a flicker of determination stirred within me. Survival instinct, perhaps, or simply the refusal to succumb to the situation without a fight.

My breaths, fogging up my goggles, became a rhythm to focus on and bring myself into the present. Each exhale was a cloud of determination, and each inhale was a draft of resolve. The night was drawing in, the temperature dropping, and I knew that time was not on my side.

Summoning every ounce of strength, I attempted to move, to somehow free myself from the grip of the snow and the broken branches. But the pain was too intense, a clear signal from my body that my injuries were beyond what sheer willpower could overcome. The panic threatened to engulf me again, a tide of hopelessness at realizing my helplessness.

Lying there, face down in the snow, the vast, indifferent sky above me, I understood the fragility of life, the thin line between adventure and misfortune. For all its beauty, the wilderness was unforgiving, a realm where human resilience was tested against the elements and the unforeseen.

Surrendering the forest to the night, I clung to the hope that rescue would come. However, it was a Wednesday night, midweek, and the trails were empty of snowmobiles. But I clung to the hope that my absence would be noted. I thought of my friends and my faithful dog. I knew no one back at the cabin would be waiting except Keslo.

I was in a very confined position facedown without the ability to move at all. Trapped in the embrace of the cold snow, my body was immobilized. I faced the longest night of my life. The darkness around me deepened, a physical manifestation of the fear and uncertainty that gripped me.

Confined in a position that allowed no movement, the harsh reality of my situation settled in with a weight heavier than the snow that blanketed me. Time stretched into an endless expanse for more than twelve hours, each minute a testament to my struggle for survival.

My body was numb, succumbing to the cold that seeped into my bones, but my mind felt the true chill of despair. More than that, processing what had happened to me was weightier.

I have never considered myself a religious man. The rituals and doctrines of faith never found a home within me. Yet, at that moment, under the vast expanse of the starlit sky, I found myself reaching out to something greater than myself.

It was not a prayer in the traditional sense but a plea, a conversation with the unseen force that I hoped watched over us all. In the face of the consuming darkness, I sought comfort in the belief of a protecting presence, a guardian in the unseen.

The night, with its oppressive silence and creeping cold, was indeed frightening. Yet, as I lay there, my voice was the only sound in the stillness, and I drew strength from the thoughts of the people I love. I spoke aloud, my words a lifeline cast into the darkness, reaching out to my children, telling them stories, imparting lessons, and expressing the love I feared I might not get another chance to share.

My laughter, though strained, broke the silence as I imagined the animals of the forest pausing in their nocturnal activities to listen to the ramblings of a stranded snowmobiler.

And to Kelso, my faithful companion waiting back at the cabin, I offered my apologies, speaking into the void with a hope that somehow, my words would bridge the distance between us.

"I'm sorry, buddy," I whispered into the cold air. "I didn't mean to leave you in the dark alone."

Imagining his confusion, his loyal heart waiting by the door for a master who would not return tonight, I felt a pang of guilt sharper than the cold.

As the hours passed, my conversations with the absent listeners ended, too. However, a while ago, they were a way to keep the encroaching despair at bay. I spoke of memories, hopes for the future, the mundane and the profound. These monologues were delivered to the night for connection and assurance that we are not alone, even in our darkest moments.

The night wore on, a seemingly endless cycle of fear, hope, and determination. My body, though numb and immobile, was alive with the will to survive, to return to those I spoke of with such longing. The cold that threatened to claim me was fought with the warmth of the thoughts of my loved ones, a mental barrier against the physical freeze.

I made desperate attempts to summon help through modern means.

"Hey, Siri," I yelled, hoping beyond hope that the voice-activated assistant on my iPhone might connect me to the outside world and summon rescue to my isolated patch of wilderness. But Siri, ever reliant on clear, unobstructed commands, remained silent, deaf to my calls.

My helmet, a protective shell meant to safeguard my head, became a barrier to my cries for help, muffling my voice. And to compound the irony, my phone lay trapped in my jacket pocket, itself pinned beneath me, rendering my attempts futile.

I didn't know how long it would last and how long I would be stuck.

Despair crept in at least twice that night, a dark cloud that overshadowed even the instinct to survive. There were moments when the end seemed inevitable and a release. After the crash, when the adrenaline faded and shock set in,

I stopped shivering—a sign, I knew, of hypothermia's grip tightening.

Then, in the eerie calm that follows the end of shivering, I thought my time had come. My breathing became shallow, each inhale a labored effort, each exhale a whisper into the frigid air. I waited for the end, for the finality that seemed so certain, yet it did not come.

In this state, between life and the anticipation of death, my consciousness would ebb, allowing me brief respites of sleep. These moments of dozing off were short-lived. However, I would jerk awake, surprised to find myself still alive, still clinging to the thread of existence.

At one point, I held my breath as if I could hasten the end on my terms. But the instinct to breathe, to fight for life even in the face of no hope, proved stronger than the fleeting impulse to give up.

The night stretched on, a seemingly endless cycle of hope and despair, fighting for survival and wishing for release. Each time I awoke, still alive, it was a reminder that the fight was not yet over, that despite the odds, I was still here, still breathing, still a part of this world.

As the night enveloped me in its cold embrace, the vast expanse of the wilderness my only companion, I engaged in a conversation that spanned the spectrum of human emotion. It was a dialogue not with another person but with the divine, with God Himself.

In the isolation of the snow-covered forest, my voice rose and fell, a solitary beacon in the darkness, carrying the weight of my fears, hopes, and despair.

The conversation began with pleas for help. My words were imbued with the desperation of a man clinging to the edge of survival. I bargained, promised, and pleaded, my breath forming clouds in the frigid air as I sought deliverance from my predicament.

But as the hours dragged on, with no sign of rescue, my emotions deepened. Anger seeped into my words, a bitter undercurrent that colored my pleas. I railed against the injustice and cruelty of being left to die in such a cold, forgotten place. Once filled with hope, my words now carried the weight of accusation, cursing the very one I had been pleading with.

Yet, as the night deepened, my anger gave way to resignation. The cold, unyielding and relentless, sapped my strength, leaching the warmth from my body until I was left numb, a shell of the man who had set out that day.

In those moments of utter vulnerability, I found myself pleading for release, for the end to come swiftly and spare me further torment. The fear of dying alone, forgotten in the snow, became a constant companion, whispering promises of peace at the ending of this pain.

But with the first light of dawn, hope flickered once more within me. The promise of the coming day rekindled the fire of survival in my heart. I began to plead for help again, my voice cracking in the cold air as I clung to the belief that rescue would come with the daylight.

The sounds of snowmobiles echoed through the forest, passing by without a hint of stopping. Despair once more took hold. They couldn't see me, hidden as I was by the snow and the trees, and with each passing engine, my hope dwindled, replaced by a deep, pervasive sense of abandonment.

At that point, with the temperature hovering between -5 and -10 degrees, the cold was no longer just an external force; it had seeped into the very marrow of my bones, stealing the sensation from my limbs until I could no longer feel any part of my body.

The realization that I might not be saved, that my prayers might go unanswered, brought a new level of desperation. I found myself oscillating between pleading for life and begging for the release of death, torment of the soul as much as of the body.

Throughout that long night, my conversation with God, many people, and close ones was a lifeline, a means of holding onto sanity in the face of overwhelming odds. The dialogue spanned the gamut of human experience, from hope to hopelessness, anger to acceptance. In those hours, I wrestled with my faith with the notion of divine benevolence and the randomness of fate.

It was a night that tested not just my physical endurance but also the foundations of my beliefs and all I hold dear.

Chapter 2: Growing Up

I was born into a world of simple means and strong values on August 21, 1967, in Green Bay, Wisconsin. My parents, Phyllis and Robert, were hardworking folks from the working class, providing a loving, albeit modest, foundation for my upbringing. Their lives, marked by dedication and warmth, deeply influenced my early childhood, teaching me the essence of hard work and the beauty of life's quiet moments.

My early years in Northern Wisconsin were a blend of seasonal adventures and lessons learned under the vast, changing skies. Winter was a wonderland of snow that brought the neighborhood kids together for endless sledding despite the biting cold that turned noses red and fingers numb.

Returning home to the comforting aroma of my mother's cooking was the perfect end to those chilly days. When spring arrived, it was like the world around us woke up. My dad would show me how to plant seeds in our garden, each one a tiny promise of what was to come. Those moments, hands dirty from the earth, taught me patience and gave me hope for the future.

Summer was freedom. The sun extended our days, allowing for endless outdoor adventures with friends. We'd build forts, scrape knees, and relish in the simple joy of childhood, with the occasional chase after the ice cream truck, jingling coins in hand. Those days felt like they would never end.

Fall in Green Bay meant football season and the excitement of Packers games. My dad's love for the team and the sense of community it brought taught me about teamwork and belonging to something bigger than myself.

My parents were everything. My mom's kindness made our home a place of joy and comfort. Losing her to Covid in 2020 was a profound loss, reminding me of life's preciousness.

My dad, strong and silent, faced his battle with colon cancer with dignity. His strength and love for our family have become the yardsticks by which I measure my life.

Growing up, my brother Greg, who's eight years older than me, and my sister Denise, who is four years my senior, were my main playmates and partners in crime.

With our parents often at work, we spent a lot of time together, creating a bond that was part necessity, part natural affection. Mom was the heart of our home, always ready with a laugh or a comforting hug. On the other hand, Dad was a bit of a mystery to us; his long work hours made his appearances at home rare but cherished.

Our family had a unique tradition sparked by Dad's hobby of buying, fixing, and selling old houses. This meant we moved almost every two years to a new place somewhere north of Green Bay, often in the countryside. Each move was an adventure, a chance to explore new surroundings, make new friends, and, inevitably, say goodbye to old ones.

These houses, each with its own challenges and charms, were more than just projects for Dad. They taught us the value of hard work and the satisfaction of making something beautiful out of something forgotten. We learned to paint, hammer, and see potential where others saw only decay. But more than that, we learned to adapt, to find home wherever we were together.

The constant moving had its tough moments, of course. Leaving behind friends and schools could be hard, but our family's unity made those transitions easier. Apart from that, some aspects of that life were tough for each one of us. Although we were a team, facing the changes and challenges head-on, with Mom's laughter and Dad's quiet strength guiding us through.

These experiences of moving and fixing homes didn't just teach us about construction or real estate; they taught us about life from my father's point of view. They showed us that change is constant, but what really matters is the people you share it with.

Through all the moves and the new beginnings, my siblings and I learned the importance of sticking together and supporting each other, no matter where we found ourselves.

For a stretch of three years, when I was about 6, we lived on a small farm. It was a big shift from our usual life of fixing and moving houses. This farm had it all: beef cattle, pigs, chickens, and even a lively bunch of Irish Setter puppies. My days were packed with farm chores, from the dirty work of cleaning stalls to the routine of feeding chickens and playing with puppies.

Living on the farm taught me a lot about hard work and looking after others. It was clear that if you skipped your chores, things quickly went downhill. But if you kept on top of them, the farm did well. It was a simple, powerful lesson that stuck with me.

After those farm years, we switched things up again. My parents bought a small grocery store in Middle Inlet, a tiny town where everyone knew each other. Running the store introduced me to a whole new set of chores. I was in charge of stocking the coolers with soda and beer, ensuring everything looked neat and inviting. I also cleaned the minnow tank for the bait shop and bagged ice, which always froze my hands.

Working in the store was different from working on the farm. It was less about caring for animals and more about serving people. I learned how to interact with customers, the importance of keeping the shelves tidy, and how satisfying it can be to organize a display just right. The store became a central spot for the community, where people came not just to shop but to catch up on news and share stories.

Living in Middle Inlet and other small towns taught me a lot about community. In places where the population barely reaches 500, everyone's contribution matters. Whether on the farm or in the store, my family found ways to fit into these communities, learning how important it is to connect with others and support each other.

Those years, moving from the farm to running the store, were full of lessons and memories. They showed me the many sides of life, the value of hard work, and the strength of community connections. These experiences from my childhood have shaped me in countless ways, guiding me through life with lessons in responsibility, diligence, and the importance of being part of a community.

Growing up, my imagination ran wild with toy tractors and model cars. I'd spend hours building and playing with models of semi-trucks, airplanes, and hot rod cars, creating my little worlds at the store. These hobbies weren't just pastimes; they were my first steps into a world of creativity and craftsmanship, inspired by the rural landscapes and machinery surrounding me.

The freedom of rural life extended beyond my imaginative play. I loved riding my bicycle around the farm, feeling a sense of adventure with every pedal. As I got older, this love for bikes naturally evolved into a passion for dirt bikes.

Racing through the fields and dirt tracks, I dreamed of speed and competition. Motocross and BMX racing became my new obsession, fueling my dreams of becoming a star racer, my name known among those who valued speed and daring.

Music also played a huge role in my life, becoming my constant companion through the ups and downs. My taste in music was wide, from rock to metal. I found a special connection with punk and alternative bands like Social Distortion in my 20s and Rise Against a little later. Full of raw emotion and energy, the music back then was a perfect fit for the rebellious spirit of a farm kid dreaming of bigger things. It was a source of comfort and inspiration, helping me navigate tough times with its powerful messages and melodies.

As I grew older, my aspirations shifted from the thrill of motocross racing to dreams of driving trucks across the country and a more grounded desire to become a firefighter. Each dream was influenced by my experiences and the values I'd learned growing up on the farm—hard work, courage, and a sense of adventure.

The friends I made, and especially my cousins, were a big part of my life. Moving around a lot meant I was always the new kid, but these cousin friends were a constant. They impacted my life in ways that still resonate with me. Even though I haven't seen many of them in years, the memories of our times together, playing and exploring on the farm, are treasures I carry with me.

In all, growing up on a small farm in the countryside shaped me in profound ways. My hobbies, from playing with toy tractors to racing dirt bikes, reflected the environment I was raised in—a place where freedom and adventure were just outside the door.

The friendships and bonds formed during those years, rooted in the simplicity and beauty of farm life, have left an indelible mark on my heart, reminding me of where I came from and the values that guide me forward.

In 1980, everything changed for us. My parents decided to sell the store we knew so well and move us to Marathon, Florida, right in the Keys. It felt like stepping into a whole new world, leaving behind the cold, familiar scenes of Wisconsin for the warm, sunny beaches of the Keys. This wasn't just a new chapter; it felt like starting a whole new book, especially for me as a child who was quite attached to the life he was brought up in with his friends and all the other farm stuff.

Marathon was different from anywhere we'd lived before. The islands, surrounded by the stunning blue of the ocean, were a paradise of palm trees and coral reefs.

Life here moved to the rhythm of the tides, a relaxed and unhurried pace. Days were filled with the kind of adventures we'd only dreamed of before: fishing in the clear waters, snorkeling to explore the colorful life under the sea, and just soaking up the beauty of our surroundings.

Adjusting to island life after the routine of farm chores and storekeeping was an adventure. We learned to live more in tune with nature, appreciating the simple pleasures like a beautiful sunset or a quiet morning by the sea. The people in Marathon were welcoming, sharing a sense of community tied together by the love of the ocean and this unique way of life.

My interests naturally shifted with this move, and that's the best part of childhood. The ocean became my new playground, offering endless possibilities for exploration and discovery. I picked up kayaking, tried my hand at sailing, and dove into the vibrant underwater world, each experience opening my eyes to new wonders and dreams.

The values and lessons from our life in Wisconsin didn't disappear; they just took on new forms as we adapted to our life by the sea. Our years in Marathon became a cherished chapter in our family's story, filled with memories of sunny days, ocean adventures, and the freedom of living close to the waves.

Moving from Wisconsin to the Florida Keys showed us how diverse life can be and how important it is to stay open to new experiences.

I grew up in a straightforward and happy home, where life felt perfect because of the little things - playing, hobbies, friends, and the good times. Childhood was this amazing phase where nothing else mattered except those moments of pure joy and adventure. It was truly the best part of life, simple yet filled with happiness, the kind everyone looks back on and wishes to relive. These memories come flooding back occasionally, reminding me of my parents and their efforts to give us a carefree and joyful childhood.

As I got older, I started to notice things about my parents' relationship that I hadn't seen when I was younger. It wasn't the picture-perfect partnership I had imagined. I began to see the subtle signs of tension and disagreements between them, which were probably always there but went unnoticed by my younger self.

This realization didn't spoil my childhood memories but made me see my parents in a new light. It showed me they were real people, dealing with their challenges while trying to make our home happy.

It made me realize the depth of their love and commitment to each other and our family. Seeing them as individuals with their own stories and struggles brought a new level of understanding and gratitude for everything they did for us.

Reflecting on those carefree days of childhood, with the perspective I have now, I treasure those times even more. They taught me about the simple joys of life, the importance of family, and how love can show up in many different ways.

As I move through life, the memories of those happy, uncomplicated days continue to inspire me, reminding me of the true essence of happiness and the lasting impact of a loving family despite its imperfections.

Chapter 3: Which Way to Go?

Childhood is often seen as the golden time of life, full of fun, freedom, and the joy of discovering the carefree world around us. For most kids, it's about playing outside until the streetlights come on, building forts, and enjoying the simple thrill of chasing after the ice cream truck. These moments make childhood special when worries are few and happiness is found in the simplest things.

But as I grew older, I noticed things weren't as perfect as they seemed. The arguments between my parents, which I used to ignore, began to stand out more.

As a child, you don't understand much; you are in your world, and the fantasy that revolves around the toys you treasure and the friendships is all that matters. But once you understand relationships, emotions, and reactions, things start to get complex, and that was the exact phase I entered when I saw and heard the disagreements between my parents. They tried not to fight in front of me, but often, I could hear them late at night arguing while they assumed I was fast asleep in my room.

This realization—that not everything was as carefree as I thought—was a big part of growing up for me. It didn't take away from the fun and adventures I had, but it did make me see things in a different light. I learned that life is complex and filled with good times and challenges. This forced me to mature emotionally and hide my fear at a young age.

I mostly grew up north of Green Bay, where city life and country calm meet. My childhood was filled with both fun times and tough moments. Among these, the anxiety I felt from my parents' frequent arguments cast a long shadow over my happier memories. I couldn't always understand why they fought, but it deeply affected me, making everything else seem harder.

School was another area where this anxiety showed up. Like any kid, I worried about keeping up with my studies and fitting in, but my fears about my parents' fights made these normal concerns feel even bigger. It was like I was carrying an extra burden, trying to balance school and my worries at the same time.

In 1982, my life took a big turn when my parents decided to get a divorce. After that decision, my mother flew me back to Green Bay, and I moved in with my older brother, who was just married and figuring his life out with his new wife. Instead of the sunny days in the Keys, I found myself in his basement, which felt completely different from any home I'd ever known.

His basement became my new room, a big change because I was scared of the dark. That basement was quite dark, with shadows that made my imagination run wild, especially at night. It felt like my fear of the dark got bigger down there, a constant reminder that I was no longer in the comfortable and familiar home I grew up in.

The basement was chilly, with the constant noise of the furnace and the occasional spider appearing.

Being in that dark basement was like dealing with all the other fears when my family split up. I had to learn to be brave in ways I hadn't before. It was tough, especially as a teenager, adjusting to many changes simultaneously. Despite these challenges, I leaned on one of the strengths I had developed as a kid: being good at following instructions.

Whether cleaning up, doing dishes, or caring for the dogs in the past, I did what was needed without complaint. This helped me get through living in my brother's basement and showed my appreciation for his support.

During these years, I didn't have much guidance from my parents. It was tough not having someone to turn to for advice on the everyday stuff, let alone the big life decisions. My brother stepped up and helped when he could, so I wasn't completely unprepared for this kind of independence.

Growing up, I had always been involved in whatever my family was doing, whether it was working on the farm or helping out in the grocery store. Those experiences taught me a lot about being responsible and taking care of things independently.

We moved a lot, so I was often the new kid at school. This wasn't easy, especially since I was nerdy and shy. Every time we moved to a new place in northern Wisconsin, or even when we lived in Florida for a bit, I had to face the challenge of walking into a new school, trying to make friends and fit in all over again.

Throughout my school years, I floated academically in the lower middle of the pack. I wasn't the star student, but I wasn't struggling at the bottom either. My life in school was more than just about grades; it was filled with the ups and downs of playing sports, hanging out with friends, and finding those subjects that genuinely sparked my interest.

Football, basketball, and a couple of years of dabbling in baseball filled my afternoons, giving me a sense of belonging and achievement outside the classroom.

There were subjects I genuinely enjoyed and looked forward to. Biology, or science in general, was one of them. My interest in the subject was largely thanks to Mr. Sroda, a teacher whose passion for science was contagious. He had a way of making the subject come alive, turning complex topics into fascinating stories. In his classes, I felt most engaged and eager to learn and explore the wonders of the natural world.

Sociology, civics, and computer classes also captured my attention. Despite my efforts, math remained a puzzle I couldn't quite solve in school. It wasn't for lack of trying; somehow, the numbers and equations never clicked for me the way concepts in biology or sociology did.

The gap in my understanding of math widened as the months went by, and by the time I realized the extent of my struggles, it felt too late to catch up. This struggle with math cast a shadow over my otherwise average academic performance, adding a layer of frustration and anxiety to my school days. It was a challenge that I never quite overcame despite my best efforts.

Not only did the tough childhood and early age problems that I had to deal with impact my mental well-being, but they also started showing their mark on my physical well-being.

I started getting really bad headaches, which I later found out were migraines. These weren't just regular headaches; they were intense and would knock me out for hours. Looking back, I think all the stress probably caused them and the worry I felt about things in my life that I couldn't change, like moving so often and my parents' troubles.

Even though, as I stated before, I'm not very religious, I've always believed in God. This belief gave me a lot of comfort during the hard times. It wasn't about following specific religious practices for me; it was more about feeling like there was something bigger out there, something that helped me stay strong when I was struggling.

These ideas from my childhood – about treating people well, staying true to myself, and having faith –helped me as I grew up. They didn't make all the problems go away, like my migraines or the stress from moving and family issues, but they gave me a way to handle them better. As I went through all the ups and downs of growing up, remembering what my family taught me and holding onto my belief in something greater helped me keep going.

By the time I was 17, I took a big step and rented an apartment with a couple of friends from high school. It was our place, and even though we were figuring things out as we went along, it felt like a real start to becoming independent.

At 17, with the end of high school looming like a giant question mark, I found myself at a crossroads, trying to pick a path into the future. It wasn't just about choosing a career; it felt like choosing who I wanted to be. But with a family that had fallen apart and a trust in the world that felt as broken as my home life, making this decision was like finding a maze without a map.

Living in an apartment with two of my buddies, I had stepped into the independence era. We were three teenagers pretending we had it all figured out when, in reality, we were trying to make it through each day. Between paying rent and keeping the fridge somewhat filled, I had to think about life after high school.

It was a mix of fun and real-life lessons. We were three teenagers figuring out how to manage rent, groceries, and all the other stuff that comes with living independently. It was exciting but also a bit scary, trying to balance being responsible with enjoying our youth.

Everyone around me seemed to have a plan, a direction, a dream they were chasing. Even my girlfriend Beth, later becoming my wife, knew what she was going to do. Me? I felt lost in a sea of options, none of which seemed to fit just right.

Then, a while after this, I decided to join the Air Force in 1987.

Funny story: when I went to the recruiting center to pick a branch, the Air Force recruiter was the only one not out grabbing lunch. So, I thought, "Why not?" and signed up immediately. I was pretty nervous about the whole thing, not gonna lie, but something inside me felt like it was the right move.

I did my technical training at Lowry Air Force Base in Denver, Colorado. They had me working on the weapons systems for the B1 bomber, which was pretty cool since we were the first class ever to do that. But it wasn't just about the B1. I learned about the weapons on all the fighter and bomber planes the Air Force had, like the F15, F16, A10, and even the big guys like the B-52. They taught us everything from loading conventional and nuclear weapons to checking the electrical systems for stray voltage and ensuring the computers and weapons were talking to each other right.

And what came next was my posting to Grand Forks Air Force Base in North Dakota. I had mixed feelings about heading out there—excited for the new start but anxious about leaving everything familiar. Still, with the training I'd had, I felt prepared.

I married Beth in 1988 while in the Air Force. We lived on the base for about three years. Being so far from home (Green Bay) was hard on both of us. We missed family and friends and returned as much as we could. Living on a military base in the middle of a corn field, with over 12,000 other people from around the US, was an experience we did not expect. But we managed to make it through. I was busy learning about military life, and she went to college at Grand Forks.

My stint in the Air Force, kicking off with that spur-of-the-moment decision and running through the intense training in Denver, set me on a new path. Heading to North Dakota, I was ready to take on whatever the Air Force had in store for me, armed with many new skills and confidence.

After all the ups and downs of joining the Air Force and getting through the tough training, things finally started to click for me at Grand Forks. It felt like I was beginning to get the hang of this adulting thing.

Deciding to join the Air Force in 1987 was by chance, but now, looking back, it was a good move. It threw me into wild experiences, from learning all about bombers in Denver to dealing with those crazy cold North Dakota winters.

1990 I was honorably discharged from the Air Force and moved back to Green Bay, Wisconsin. I worked odd jobs for a while.

I remember thinking about different careers. Once, inspired by a buddy from the Air Force who was into firefighting, I toyed with the idea of becoming a firefighter myself. It seemed cool, but I didn't stick with the idea for long.

A while later, Beth and I were just out for a walk when I passed the Allouez Fire Department and saw they were looking for paid on-call firefighters. Deciding to become a firefighter wasn't just a random choice. It resulted from all the searching and all the living I'd done up to that point.

I found myself at another major crossroads in my life. I'd gotten a taste of what it was like to be a paid-on-call firefighter, and it resonated with me. Something about rushing toward danger instead of away from it, about being there for people on their worst day, just clicked with me. It felt right in a way that was hard to ignore. So, I made up my mind: firefighting wouldn't just be a side gig; it would be my career.

Starting as a paid on-call firefighter was the beginning of something big for me. It wasn't just about starting a career but finding my path, which clicked with who I was and what I wanted to do.

Now, I had options. There was this tempting path to work for a military aircraft contractor. It would've meant packing up and moving to Washington State or some other place where the military had its contractors set up. It was a job that would've used my Air Force experience directly. But, when I weighed it against the life of a firefighter, the choice became surprisingly clear.

So, after some time, I enrolled in EMT school and completed the course. I also joined the De Pere Fire Department as a paid on-call Firefighter. I enrolled in Fox

Valley Technical College to become a fire protection technician. It was a two-year associate degree program.

My time at Fox Valley Technical College was about more than just getting a piece of paper. The program covered everything from the nitty-gritty technical skills to understanding fire behavior and safety protocols – all that was relevant once I started working full-time. I had the opportunity to put the knowledge I gained here to the test in real situations.

The funny thing is that I landed a full-time firefighter job before finishing my degree. But there was no way I was going to drop out. I stuck with it, knowing that every class and every exam was getting me closer to my goal of joining the Green Bay Fire Department.

Landing a job while still in school was kind of tough. It meant balancing work with classes and applying what I learned in real-time at Antigo Fire Department full-time as a firefighter. When I finally graduated with my diploma in hand, I felt ready for anything. All this prepared me for my eventual career with the Green Bay Fire Department, which was my ultimate goal.

Becoming a firefighter was a dream come true, but it was just the beginning of a journey with plenty more twists, turns, and adventures in store.

Then, training in the Green Bay Fire Department was an everyday thing, blending hands-on experience with formal learning. Every day brought new lessons, whether through structured sessions or real-life calls. We covered it all - firefighting strategies, medical emergencies, using tools to free people from wrecked cars, treating injuries, and even how to drive emergency vehicles safely and effectively.

My college years and EMT training drilled into me the importance of managing emergency scenes calmly and effectively. Being able to stay calm and make smart decisions amid chaos helps to provide the best possible outcome and earn the trust and cooperation of those you're helping. This idea of maintaining composure and treating people with respect during their worst moments was invaluable.

The skills and mindset I developed from my training were crucial during the toughest night of my life, helping me stay calm and assess my injuries, and ultimately, they played a huge part in getting me through it.

Choosing firefighting meant choosing the kind of life I wanted to lead. The idea of being part of a close-knit team, of diving into the fray to save lives and protect property, had a pull that no contractor gig could match.

Chapter 4: A New Phase

Going back to '88 again, life took a pretty sweet turn when I married. My now ex-wife and I met during high school initially. Fast forward a bit, we were blessed with two amazing kids, Nicholas and Madison, who are now 28 and 26, respectively. Having them 18 months apart meant they grew up close, which was awesome. As a dad, I was all about showing them the ropes of life, emphasizing the importance of family, getting along, and pitching in wherever needed.

Being involved in their lives, especially in sports, was something I took to heart. I dove into coaching, taking on basketball and football for Nick and softball for Maddie. Volleyball was in the mix, too, though they had that pretty well covered with other coaches.

Through all this, I aimed to teach them about teamwork and dedication. I always said, *"If you're going to start a sport, you're sticking with it till the season's over. No quitting!!"*

It was about teaching them to commit and showing them the value of being part of a team.

I made it a point to be there for them, whether it was practices or games, no matter what. Working 24-hour shifts at the fire department meant I had to get creative with my schedule, trading shifts to ensure I didn't miss their tournaments and games. And honestly, I wouldn't have had it any other way.

Summers were our time to shine. I went all out to ensure Nick and Maddie had the best breaks from school. We went camping, took trips, spent days fishing – you name it. Keeping them active and engaged was my goal, and judging by the smiles and laughter, I'd say mission accomplished.

Through all these adventures and moments spent together, I hoped to instill in them a sense of pride, the importance of teamwork, and the joy of staying active and embracing life, I can most proudly say that I was successful in doing that.

Watching them grow into the wonderful, respectful adults they are today has been one of my greatest joys. And while life has had its ups and downs, those moments coaching their teams, cheering from the sidelines, and exploring the great outdoors together are the times I cherish the most.

Fast forward a bit to now, my son, Nick, has made a life for himself out in Washington State. He's working at a resort called Stevens Pass, a Vail resort, a dream come true for someone who loves the outdoors as much as he does.

Then there's my daughter, Madison, or as we call her, Maddie. She's 26 and has recently started a new chapter of her life with her husband, Alex. They got married in July 2023 and decided to settle down in Longmont, Colorado, with their dog, Luca, who's pretty much like a child to them. Maddie's taken her passion for helping others and turned it into a career as a social worker, living just outside Boulder, where the mountains are practically in her backyard.

Nick and Maddie are incredible people; honestly, saying I'm proud of them is an understatement. They've both got this amazing drive and a love for life that just doesn't quit.

Nick's been with Vail Corporation for almost eight years, thriving in the ski resort world, while Maddie and Alex are all about the great outdoors. They're always off camping or hiking whenever they get the chance.

Speaking of hiking, Maddie and Alex recently tackled the Colorado Trail. We're talking about a journey of over 500 miles, which they completed in 40 days. Just thinking about that kind of adventure blows my mind. It's not just the physical challenge but the sheer dedication and love for nature it takes to embark on something like that.

My bond with my kids is strong; we talk often and catch up whenever possible. Despite the distance, our reunions felt like we were never apart. Traveling to see them sometimes is difficult, but we make it work. They're busy building their lives and relationships, but I hope they'll move closer to Wisconsin someday.

Watching my kids become the adults they are today has been my life's greatest joy. They're not just living their lives; they're grabbing life by the horns and making the most of every moment. They've grown into respectful, contributing members of society who've taken the values we've tried to instill in them and put them into action.

Their love for the outdoors, commitment to their work and each other, and ability to face challenges head-on are just a few of the things that make me so proud to be their dad.

Reflecting on all this, it's clear that the adventures we shared in their childhood and my era as a present father had led them somewhere, and the times spent together have all played a part in shaping who they've become. And as they continue to write their own stories, exploring the world and making their mark, I can't help but feel excited to see where their paths will lead them next.

Life, as it turns out, has its share of twists and turns. At the beginning of February 2022, my then-wife, Beth, and I decided to go our separate ways. At that point, she was still living in Colorado, a place we had called home together for a while. Meanwhile, I had already made the move back to Wisconsin in 2021. It was one of those life changes you don't see coming, but you must face it head-on when it arrives.

Our time in Colorado, lasting about two and a half years, was a chapter filled with its own stories, adventures, and learning curves. Living there, amidst the mountains and the vast outdoor life that both my kids now thrive in, was an experience in itself. It's a place that can change your perspective, with its breathtaking landscapes and the sense of freedom you feel just being out in the wild. But the state didn't feel like home to me, and as life would have it, not all chapters are meant to last forever.

Despite the separation and the miles between us, my bond with my kids, Nick and Maddie, remains unbreakable. It's one of those silver linings in situations that otherwise feel pretty tough. We've managed to maintain a strong, positive relationship, navigating this new dynamic with openness and understanding. It's not always easy, but it's worth every effort.

The move back to Wisconsin, while initially a bit of a culture shock after living in Colorado, felt right. It was a return to familiar ground, to roots that run deep. In many ways, it's given me the chance to reconnect with myself, to reflect on the journey so far, and to look forward to what's coming next.

With its mountains, challenges, and beauty, life in Colorado will always be a part of me. It's a place and a time that contributed significantly to who I am today.

This transition from being married and living in Colorado to being single and back in Wisconsin has been a journey of its own. There are moments of nostalgia, sure, memories of times spent exploring the great outdoors with the family, memories that are as vivid as ever. But it's also a reminder that no matter what life throws your way, the bonds that matter most can weather any storm.

As I look back on the time spent in Colorado and on all the chapters that have unfolded since, I'm grateful for every experience and lesson learned. Life is a collection of moments, change, and growth.

After hanging up my helmet and retiring from the Green Bay Fire Department in July 2018, life took me on a detour out to Colorado. But, as fate would have it, I found myself back in Wisconsin four months before a significant turn of events. Coming back, I had a clear goal: I wanted to return to the workforce, but this time in a completely different field from firefighting. The paper-making industry had always caught my interest, partly because my dad had spent some years working in it, leaving me with a curiosity about the craft and a desire to follow in his footsteps, at least in some capacity.

With this goal in mind, I set my sights on a local paper mill where I felt I could start a new chapter and sink my teeth into learning something entirely new. That's when I landed a position at Georgia Pacific Paper Mill in Green Bay. My role was as a machine operator. It was a whole new world compared to the adrenaline-fueled days and nights of firefighting, but it was exactly the change I sought.

Working at the mill meant diving into paper-making, a fascinating and complex process. The job came with its own set of challenges and learning curves, but I was all in. My schedule was a shift rotation of four 12-hour shifts followed by four days off. Then, it changed to two-day shifts followed by two-night shifts.

This rhythm, while demanding, offered a balance that allowed me to dedicate myself fully to the job during my days and then take some time to recharge and enjoy life on my days off.

Being a machine operator at the paper mill wasn't just about clocking in and out; it was about becoming part of a tradition that stretched back generations in Green Bay, a city known for its paper industry. It was about contributing to a process that turned raw materials into products used by people all over the world. And for me, it was about connecting to a part of my family history, to a line of work my father had known and contributed to.

The decision to work there, to immerse myself in the paper-making industry, was driven by a mix of personal interest and a desire for a new challenge.

After years of serving the community as a firefighter, this was my chance to learn, grow, and contribute in a different field. It was an opportunity to start fresh, to build new skills, and to see where this next phase of my career would take me.

So, as I adjusted to my new role at the paper mill, I couldn't help but feel excited about the possibilities. This wasn't just about filling my days or keeping busy but fulfilling a longtime curiosity. With each shift and rotation, I learned the ins and outs of paper-making and weaving my story.

As I moved forward with my new life, I looked forward to the learning and experiences ahead. It was a testament to the idea that it's never too late to try something new, to shift gears, and to find fulfillment in unexpected places. As I settled into my routine, working my shifts and enjoying my days off, I knew that this chapter, while different from anything I'd done before, was an important part of my journey.

Switching gears from the high-octane life of a firefighter to the routine of a machine operator at the paper mill meant a whole new kind of busyness. Those 12-hour shifts were no joke; they left me pretty wiped by the end of the day. So, my after-work routine became pretty simple: grab some food, maybe zone out in front of the TV for a bit, or tackle a few errands if I had any juice left. That was all I could manage before hitting the sack and doing it again the next day.

But those four days off?

That's when the real magic happened. I'd head to my cabin in Townsend, Wisconsin, about 80 miles north of Green Bay. Beth and I repurchased it about ten years ago. That place was my slice of heaven, my perfect escape from the grind. Up there, it was all about enjoying the great outdoors, no matter the season.

Spring through fall, you'd find me zipping around the trails on my UTV, kicking up dust and taking in the fresh air. Come winter, I'd swap the UTV for a snowmobile, tearing through the snow-covered landscape with that same sense of freedom and adventure. Those days off were my time to recharge and live life at a different pace.

Hanging out with friends became a cabin staple, too. We'd hit up a local bar and grill for a burger, share stories, and relax. The cabin was also a great spot for tackling projects, whether fixing something in the garage or making improvements. And let's not forget about bowhunting — something about being out in the quiet woods, waiting for the perfect shot, that's incredibly grounding.

Taking walks with my dog, Kelso, was another highlight. There's something special about wandering through the woods with your four-legged buddy by your side: no agenda, no rush. Just the two of you and nature. Those walks were the perfect way to clear my head and appreciate the simple things.

So, while the workdays at the mill were all about focus and getting the job done, my days off at the cabin were a whole different story. They were about making the most of my time, indulging in my hobbies, spending quality moments with my friend Kelso, and enjoying nature. It was a balance that worked for me, a rhythm that kept me going through the busy workweeks.

This routine, this way of dividing my time between the demands of work and the joys of life at the cabin, became my new normal. And honestly, I wouldn't have it any other way.

It was a life that allowed me to experience the best of both worlds: the satisfaction of a hard day's work and the freedom to enjoy the simple pleasures of cabin life. However, I didn't even know that something so huge could happen that could switch the gears of my life again.

Chapter 5: Like Any Other Day

And just like that, I had found my rhythm, a perfect blend of work and wilderness, each aspect fueling my spirit in different yet complementary ways.

The cabin in Townsend became more than just a retreat; it was a sanctuary where I could reconnect with the essence of who I was, away from the noise and demands of the everyday. It was where I felt most alive, whether navigating the trails on my UTV, weaving through the snow on my snowmobile, or simply enjoying the tranquility of nature with Kelso by my side.

Life had settled into a comfortable pace, predictable yet fulfilling in its simplicity and the joys it brought. While demanding, my time at the Paper Mill provided a sense of accomplishment and purpose, a way to engage with the community and contribute to something bigger than myself. Also something that I had always wished to do from the beginning, just like my father.

Meanwhile, the cabin offered a chance to unwind, live in the moment, and cherish the adventures of each changing season.

Both old and new friends became an integral part of my life, their laughter and stories adding color to the canvas of my days when I resided there. Whether we were sharing a meal at the local bar and grill, tackling a new project around the cabin, or hitting the trails on the snowmobile.

Yet, as content as I was with this delicate balance I had struck, life reminded me that change is the only true constant. Just when I thought I had it all figured out, an event loomed on the horizon, poised to shift the gears of my life in a way I never could have anticipated. It reminded us that we ultimately do not control all our planning and routines.

The day of the crash fell right in the middle of my days off—day three of four, to be precise. It was Wednesday, February 23rd, 2022, a notably chilly day in Wisconsin, with nighttime temperatures plunging well below zero. Despite the cold, the lure of the snow-covered trails was too strong to resist, a perfect backdrop for an adventure with friends.

I left my cabin a little after noon, eager for the day's escapades. My good friends Brian and Al were with me, and we were on our snowmobiles, ready to tackle the winter landscape. We set off, the cold air biting but invigorating, as we made our way north, the engines of our sleds growling beneath us.

Our first stop was a gas station, a predetermined meeting point where we joined up with a third friend. The camaraderie was tangible, and the excitement for the day's ride was noticeable among us. Not long after, about an hour further north along the trail, our group expanded to include one more friend.

Together, we made a solid crew, sharing laughs and building stories as we zoomed across the snowy terrain, the freedom of the ride heightening the sense of adventure.

We rode all day, the hours slipping as we traversed the trails, lost in the moment's joy. The cold was a mere afterthought, secondary to the thrill of speeding over the snow and the companionship of good friends. Yet, as the afternoon faded into evening, a sense of duty nudged me; it was time to head back. Kelso was waiting for me back at the cabin, and I couldn't let him down.

The journey south back to my cabin was a familiar route I had taken many times before. But this time, something was different. Something was going to be different. As I navigated the snowmobile along the trail, heading towards home, the unexpected loomed ahead, a twist of fate on an otherwise ordinary day of winter fun.

Little did I know, as I sped through the snowy landscape, that this ride would be unlike any other. The events about to unfold would mark this day in my memory forever, a stark reminder of how quickly life can change. As I pushed on, focused on the trail ahead and the warmth of home just a ride away, the next chapter of my story would begin—a chapter that would test me in ways I never imagined.

Chapter 6: Deep in the Snow

The next thing I knew, a wild and unpredictable deer darted across my path, its timing perfectly aligned with my snowmobile's trajectory. The collision, whether the doe hit my sled or hit my body, shattered the quiet of the winter evening in an instant. I was airborne briefly before landing with a thud, the world around me silenced by the snow. Lying there, face down in the freezing blanket that covered the ground, time seemed to slow down. It had been over half an hour or more since I landed, and with each passing minute, the cold deepened, seeping into my bones.

For the first hour, my instincts kicked in full force. I screamed and yelled for help, hoping against hope that someone would hear me and that rescue was on its way.

But as minutes ticked by, the realization set in—help wasn't coming. The rush of adrenaline that initially flooded my body, masking the pain and the cold, began to wane, and the true extent of my situation started to dawn on me. The cold, which had been at bay, now wrapped its icy fingers around me, though in those moments, the shock was so intense that I barely registered the freezing temperatures.

Crashing into the deer and then the trees felt almost surreal, a bizarre echo of the minor accidents I'd had before like those times I crashed on my dirt bike and walked away with just a few bruises. This, however, was different. It was like that split second when you stub your toe—there's a brief, eerie pause before the pain hits, and you know it's only a matter of time before the real agony starts. Or, like when you get the wind knocked out of you, you think, 'Just give me a minute, I'll be fine,' but deep down, you know it's not that simple.

Lying there, I couldn't help but think back to those moments of resilience, bouncing back up after a fall. But this was no dirt bike race, and the cold, unforgiving ground beneath me offered no quick reprieve. The temperature that night, hovering around -7F, was the harsh reality of a northern Wisconsin winter.

The cold wasn't just a backdrop to my predicament; it was an active participant, threatening to turn a bad situation into something far worse.

As I lay there face down, and the surroundings seemed to close around me, the usual comforting silence of nature now reminded me of my isolation. The snow, which had always been a source of joy and play, now felt like a cold, wet blanket, impossible to escape.

Lying there, the dead silence even let me hear the tall trees looming with the biting air. I couldn't even look at the sky, or that could have been a relief in the pitch darkness of the night,

In those moments, time lost all meaning. The world narrowed to the immediate struggle for survival, each breath a victory against the encroaching cold and pain. The wilderness, a place I had always felt at home, now felt indifferent to human suffering. The realization that I was truly alone and that my fate rested solely in my hands was terrifying and clarifying. It was a test of will, a challenge to muster every ounce of strength I possessed.

As the shock began to wear off, I took stock of my injuries, the reality of my situation sinking in with chilling clarity. My right arm was severely broken; both bones, I assumed, snapped in a way that left no doubt about the severity of the fracture. My left arm was in no better shape, dislocated at the elbow and possibly broken, trapped at an unnatural angle beneath my body.

The numbness in my left leg was a telltale sign of a broken femur entangled in a branch, sparking fears of a potentially life-threatening bleed from a torn femoral artery. This was the nightmare scenario that played out in my mind: the possibility of bleeding out alone in the snow.

My right leg, the only source of pain initially, bore the brunt of my immediate physical discomfort. The knee area was torn up, and my hip felt like it had borne the full impact of my collision with the ground. As time crept by, an indeterminate number of minutes stretching into eternity, the pain began to spread, searing through all my extremities with a vengeance that was both overwhelming and terrifying.

Despite the mounting pain and the dire nature of my injuries, I found a sliver of hope in the realization that my head, neck, and back seemed unharmed. Tentatively, I began to move these areas, testing for any hint of pain or restriction.

The relief that flooded me was a bit easing when I found none, granting me a small measure of comfort amid agony.

It was a grim consolation, the thought that avoiding injury to these critical areas might spare me a quicker demise, coupled with the knowledge that I had remained conscious throughout the ordeal. My extremities might have been battered and broken, but my core, my vital center, remained intact.

Lying there, face down in the snow, the environment around me was surreal. The once-familiar woods felt alien, a silent witness to my struggle. Initially held at bay by adrenaline, the cold began to assert itself with an insidious persistence. The snow beneath me, soft and yielding at first, now felt like a frozen shroud, leeching the warmth from my body with every passing minute.

The trees, their branches laden with snow, must have stood tall and indifferent around me while the pain and fear consumed me and increased every minute. The night sky must've been a canopy of stars overhead, but it offered no comfort as my vision was quite limited, and I was stuck face down.

The quiet of the winter woods, usually a peaceful respite, now amplified the severity of my situation, each rustle and whisper of wind a taunt in the face of my immobility and made me desperate to hear something that could offer some form of help.

The boundary between minutes and hours blurred as I lay trapped, caught in a limbo of pain and uncertainty. Yet, even as despair threatened to take hold, a part of me clung to hope, the possibility of rescue and survival.

I lay there, and the cascade of thoughts running through my mind was relentless. It's crucial to walk through the timeline of that night, from the initial shock of the impact to the ensuing panic, the creeping in of pain, and the multitude of emotions that ebbed and flowed over the next 12 hours. It's a sequence that paints a vivid picture of the ordeal, allowing the reader to journey alongside me through those dark and painful hours.

The first-hour post-impact was a blur of trying to grasp the extent of my injuries and my situation, but as time wore on, the grim possibility of not making it out alive began to dominate my thoughts.

My mind raced, fluctuating wildly between the pain engulfing my body and the dire reality of my predicament. When the cold began to set in truly, it was merciless. At first, the shivering was light, almost manageable. It escalated into violent convulsions that, in a cruel twist, probably helped keep me warm, as if I were enduring a grueling workout.

Keeping calm became my primary focus, a monumental task amid the chaos of my thoughts and the pain searing through my body. I desperately tried to think of any possible way to escape my situation. Echoing the attempts from earlier, I called out for Siri repeatedly until my voice was nothing but a raspy whisper, drained of all strength.

Throughout the night, I fought to turn over or even to kneel, but as the hours passed, my limbs numbed to the point of feeling utterly non-existent, a sensation that shifted from pins and needles to nothingness.

At some point, resignation began to seep in. Armed with the knowledge from my training, I recognized I was not in shock, which gave me comfort, but the signs of hypothermia were setting in. In moments of utter despair, the thought of simply falling asleep and succumbing to the cold was almost a relief. The notion of enduring this ordeal only to freeze to death seemed, in some twisted way, preferable to the continuous struggle against the inevitable. I imagined that perhaps, in a few days, someone might stumble upon my body, bringing an end to this chapter.

Surrounded by the dense, snow-laden woods, the silence of the night was both a torment and a reminder of my isolation. The crisp winter air, once invigorating, now felt like an early call of my demise, each breath a laborious effort against the biting cold.

In the immediate aftermath of the impact, my breaths came fast and hard, as if I'd just sprinted the final stretch of a marathon. But this was no race; it was a struggle for survival. The shock of the collision had sent my body into overdrive, my heart pounding against my chest, each breath a battle. Aware of the toll this frantic breathing took, I knew I needed to slow it down to find a rhythm amidst the chaos.

The darkness of the night seemed endless, a void in which hope dwindled with each passing minute. The struggle to maintain consciousness, to cling to life despite the overwhelming odds, was a battle waged in solitude, a test of wills against the relentless elements.

Amidst the despair, there were flickers of determination and moments of clarity between the fog of pain and fear. The fight for survival, the refusal to give in without a struggle, underscored the profound instinct to live, even in the direst of circumstances.

It was a testament to our strength, often lying dormant until summoned by necessity, a strength that defines the essence of what it means to endure, hope, and persevere against all odds.

As the hours stretched endlessly into the night, a profound shift occurred. My thoughts wandered to my kids, flashbacks to our shared life, the moments that defined us—memories woven through the best and most challenging times.

Lying there in the cold, my mind raced with thoughts of what I'd miss if I didn't make it through the night. At the forefront were my kids. The pain of not being there for their milestone moments—like their weddings or meeting my future grandchildren—weighed heavily on my heart. These weren't just events but pivotal chapters of life that I desperately wanted to be part of. The thought of being absent for those moments, of leaving my kids to navigate those significant days without their dad, filled me with a sense of immense sadness.

Then, I reflected on my life with Beth, my ex-wife. The decision to separate had been tough, and in that moment of vulnerability, the weight of that choice hit me hard. Aside from my kids, it made me realize how alone I felt. No one knew where I was; no one was coming to look for me. That realization was both terrifying and isolating.

But my thoughts didn't stop with my human family; they extended to Kelso, my loyal dog waiting back at the cabin. The idea of him alone, unable to understand why I hadn't returned, broke my heart. I pictured him there, in the dark, hungry and confused, waiting by the door for a master who might never come back. It's one thing to consider the impact of our absence on those who understand the concept of loss, but the innocence of a pet, their unconditional love and dependence, brought a different kind of sorrow.

Sometime deep in the night, beyond the few initial hours post-crash, my body transitioned from a state of uncontrollable shivering to an eerie calm. It's hard to pinpoint exactly when this change took place. Still, it was as if the intense, electrifying tremors had exhausted themselves, leaving behind a stillness that felt both peaceful and ominous.

In the fire service, we have a term for when someone has passed—ADD, "all done dancing." It's a bit of dark humor we keep to ourselves, not meant for the ears of the public. Lying there in the snow, feeling the stillness take over, I couldn't help but think I was all done dancing. The analogy we once applied to others was my reality in the cold, dark forest.

My breathing slowed dramatically, becoming shallow and infrequent, starkly contrasting to the rapid, desperate gasps that had filled the earlier hours. Each breath now came at intervals that stretched longer and longer, a pattern I recognized all too well from my years of responding to emergencies. It was the kind of breathing that, in my professional experience, meant close to the end.

This realization that I might be experiencing my final moments cast a surreal pall over the situation. Once a place of adventure and freedom, the snowy landscape around me now felt like a vast, indifferent expanse, witnessing what I believed might be my last breaths in the pitch-black night.

Despite the gravity of the situation, my mind clung to the images of my children, to the life we'd built together. It was a lifeline in that darkness. The thought of not seeing them again, of leaving them with only memories, filled me with a sense of profound sadness. Yet, even as despair threatened to overwhelm me, the love I held for them provided a measure of strength, a reason to fight even as my body seemed ready to surrender.

In those moments, caught between life and death, my career as a firefighter—a life spent in the service of others, rushing toward danger when others fled—seemed to come full circle. Here I was, on the other side of the emergency, fighting a deeply personal and universally understood battle: the will to live, to hold on against seemingly insurmountable odds. It was a struggle defined not by the heroics of the job but by the raw human desire to survive, to cling to life in the face of the inevitable.

My years of training kicked in, reminding me of the importance of self-assessment and maintaining calm in the face of adversity. That training wasn't just about saving others; in that moment, it became about saving myself.

A significant change occurred as the night wore on, passing the halfway mark into the unknown hours of darkness. It was as if my body had reached a tipping point, transitioning from the frenzied breathing of someone fighting to stay afloat to the eerie calm of resignation. The shift was abrupt; after what felt like an endless cycle of rapid breaths, I took a deep sigh, a profound breath that seemed to carry all the weight of my predicament. And then, for a moment that stretched into eternity, I felt no urge to breathe again.

When my lungs finally demanded air, it was with a deliberate, measured breath, as if I was preparing to dive into the ocean's depths. A slow, intentional inhale followed by a gradual exhale. This breathing pattern was hauntingly familiar, so slow, shallow, and labored. Over my years in the fire department, I'd seen it in countless patients, a reminder of what usually came next: death. It was a sign I'd come to recognize all too well, and ironically, it was happening to me now.

The cold, which had once set my body shivering uncontrollably, now felt distant, as if I were slowly being disconnected from the physical world. The pain, fear, and uncertainty faded into the background, replaced by a strange sense of detachment. I was adrift, caught between the will to fight and accepting my fate, my life hanging in the balance.

There, beneath the indifferent expanse of stars, I found myself speaking to God with no vision in front of me apart from the haunting darkness, a continuous stream of questions and pleas.

What was next? Would I know the moment of departure, or would it be like drifting into an endless sleep, a world of dreams I wouldn't wake? The uncertainty of it all was overwhelming, yet in those moments, I sought answers, some form of understanding of what awaited on the other side.

Time, it seemed, had slowed to a crawl. Each minute felt drawn to my anticipation and readiness to face whatever came next. I had reached a point of acceptance, a strange peace with the thought of leaving behind the physical world. And so, I waited, expecting the end to come at any moment, urging it on in a bid to escape the pain and the cold that had been my constant companions since the crash.

But death did not come. Despite my attempts to hasten it, even holding my breath desperately trying to find release, life clung to me. The calm that had settled over me, the acceptance of my fate, gave way to confusion.

'Why was I still here? What purpose did I have left to fulfill?' These questions circled in my mind, unanswered.

The relief I had felt at the thought of escape from my predicament was replaced by a bewildering sense of survival. I was alive, against all odds, left to ponder the reasons why.

The crisp, cold night air seemed to carry my words away, whispering into the void. In the distance, the occasional sound of a branch snapping under the weight of the snow punctuated the silence, a reminder of the world moving on, oblivious to my plight.

In this liminal space, caught between life and death, I contemplated the value of existence and the reasons to keep fighting. The thought of my children, of the love and memories we shared, anchored me to life, a beacon of hope in the darkness. It was for them, the chance to see them again, to tell them all the things left unsaid, that I found a renewed will to survive.

As the night wore on, my battle continued a test of will against the merciless cold and the injuries that threatened to claim me. I realized then that my journey was not yet over, that there were still chapters left unwritten in the "story of my life" (which happens to be a Social Distortion song). The questions I had posed to the heavens remained unanswered, but a new resolve took root in their place. If I was still breathing, then perhaps there was more for me to do and more life to live.

The ordeal had changed me, leaving its mark in ways I could not fully comprehend. But one thing was clear: I was alive for a reason and determined to find out why.

Chapter 7: Cold and Numb

As the long night unfolded, with the cold seeping deeper into my bones and the darkness around me haunting everything even more, I grappled with frustration, desperation, and the sheer will to survive. Amidst the pain and the chilling cold, one of my few lifelines to the outside world lay just inches away, yet frustratingly out of reach – my iPhone, tucked away in my jacket pocket, my helmet muffling any attempts at communication.

As I talked about it in earlier chapters, in those moments, I called out to Siri, the digital assistant I had relied on for so many mundane tasks, now a beacon of hope in my dire situation.

But Siri remained silent, unable to hear my calls for help. The irony of the situation wasn't lost on me – technology, so integral to our daily lives, rendered useless in my moment of greatest need. Lying there, face down in the snow, my body entangled in a branch that held me captive, I couldn't help but feel a sense of betrayal.

Here I was, engaged in a life-or-death struggle, and my faithful companion, my phone, could do nothing to aid me. The helmet on my head, designed to protect me, now acted as a barrier between me and potential rescue. The frustration was a bitter reminder of my vulnerability in the face of nature's indifference.

The silence that followed each attempt to summon help was a heavyweight, adding to the already suffocating blanket of snow that enveloped me. It contrasted with the usual instant gratification of digital assistance, a sobering realization of how quickly we can be cut off from the AI world we take for granted.

As the night wore on, my anger at Siri, irrational as it might seem, became a focal point for my thoughts. It was somehow easier to direct my frustration at a piece of technology than to fully confront the gravity of my situation.

Each failed attempt to activate Siri reminded me of my isolation, of the vast distance between myself and any hope of rescue. My visibility was limited to the small patch of ground immediately before me; my world was reduced to snow, darkness, and the faint outline of branches against the night sky.

The realization that I was utterly alone, that the digital world I was so connected to could offer no assistance was a sobering thought. It underscored the fragility of our existence, the thin line that separates every day from the extraordinary, the safe from the perilous.

Despite the hopelessness of my attempts, I continued to call out, the sound of my voice a small comfort in the overwhelming silence. It was the human spirit, the refusal to give in even when faced with the odds of the situation. My anger at Siri, the situation, and the cruel twist of fate that had led me here simmered beneath the surface, a flicker of emotion in the numbing cold.

In this silence of the wilderness, I found myself engaging in a conversation unlike any I had before. As I mentioned before, I'm not a man of religious conviction, but the extremity of my situation drove me to reach out to a higher power, to the concept of a protective presence I hoped existed.

In the depths of my solitude and despair, I began talking to God. It was a dialogue born out of desperation, clutching at any possibility for solace. My voice, weak and raspy from the cold and exertion, broke the silence of the night with whispers and pleas directed at the heavens.

The thought of missing out on my kids' future achievements, their joys and sorrows, and the milestones yet to come was unbearable. Each mention of my kids brought a fresh wave of determination, an intense wish to be spared, and the opportunity to see them grow and be there for them as I always had been.

But as the night wore on, my requests mingled with anger and frustration—anger at finding myself in this predicament, frustration at the seeming silence in response to my pleas. There were moments when I questioned everything: the fairness of life, the existence of a mighty force watching over us. Yet, even in those moments of doubt, I continued to speak into the void, clinging to the sliver of hope that my words were being heard.

The cold that had once set my body shivering uncontrollably now seemed to recede into the background, replaced by a different kind of chill—emanating from realizing my vulnerability and my hold on life. It was a confrontation with my mortality, the limits of human endurance, and the unseen forces that govern our fate.

The stillness of the night was occasionally broken by the distant call of a nocturnal creature or the creaking of a tree branch under the weight of the snow, and each sound was a reminder of the life that persisted around me, oblivious to my plight. These fleeting disturbances only served to underscore the isolation of my circumstances, the contrast between the vibrancy of the natural world and the desperate, singular battle for survival that I was engaged in.

Throughout this long night of the soul, my appeals to a higher power alternated between requests for release and rescue, between accepting my fate and a fierce unwillingness to let go. The cold, the pain, and the fear became the backdrop to an intensely personal journey through the landscape of my beliefs and convictions, a journey marked not by visible milestones but by the ebb and flow of hope and despair.

This cycle of thoughts and emotions continued on and on throughout the night. I now look back and think this is what it means to reach deep into your soul. To where my heart and brain come together and decide to keep pushing forward or accept my fate and give in.

As the night went on, I felt anger and sadness. I was mad at everything - the situation I was in, and yes, even at God. Being stuck in the snow, unable to move, all I could do was feel mad. The trees around me, which I usually liked, now seemed to mock me with their whispers in the wind. Another thing that annoyed me was the darkness surrounding me and the branch that stuck to me and couldn't let me move.

But the anger didn't last forever. It faded, leaving me wishing for everything just to end. I started to think a lot about what happens after you die.

Would I just go to sleep and not wake up?

Would I know when I was about to die?

These thoughts kept spinning in my head, but no answers came. I kept waiting for death to take me away, but it didn't happen. Eventually, I gave up, hoping for anything.

Yet, in the back of my mind, I kept thinking about my kids, my family, and all the things left unsaid and undone. Those thoughts kept pulling me back, making me wish for a way out of this mess. I talked out loud to my kids, hoping somehow they'd know I was thinking of them. I even talked to my dog, Kelso, feeling sorry he was alone in the cabin. Even though no one could hear me, talking like this made me feel a bit better.

This talking became very important to me. It helped me not to feel so alone. I imagined telling my kids everything I wanted to say, joking that even the animals around might be listening. This made me feel connected to life outside my snowy trap. It reminded me why I still wanted to live - to fix things and make more memories.

Hour after hour, I fought between wanting to give up and wanting to live for those small, important reasons. It was hard, but those thoughts of my family and dog gave me a little hope in the dark.

But talking to God, my kids, Kelso, and even imagining the animals listening made me hold on. It showed me that even when things are terrible, some of us want to keep going, to get back to the people and things we love.

As the first light of dawn began to break the grip of the night, my spirits lifted ever so slightly. The darkness that had me in isolation was now giving way to the soft light of morning, painting the snow around me with a pale glow. This change, this transition from night to day, sparked a renewed sense of hope within me. Maybe, just maybe, this new light meant I would be seen; perhaps rescue was close at hand.

I started to plead for help again, this time with a sense of urgency fueled by the breaking dawn.

"Help!" I shouted as loudly as my injuries allowed, hoping that the increasing visibility would bring someone, anyone, to my aid.

The thought that perhaps God had finally heard my pleas and was sending help filled me with a mixture of hope and desperation. As dawn broke, it felt like a promise that my ordeal might end.

Yet, as the minutes ticked by and the silence remained unbroken except for the natural sounds of the morning, my initial surge of optimism began to wane. The cold still clung to me, a relentless reminder of my situation. The snow that had felt like a prison overnight now seemed to taunt me with its brightness while dark thoughts once again began to cloud my mind.

I tried to scan my surroundings, turning my head as much as my injuries would allow, searching for any sign of movement, any indication that help was on the way, but all I could see was the snow and branches surrounding me.

With each passing moment, the reality of my situation settled in deeper. I was still alone, still trapped, and the path to my rescue was as uncertain as ever.

I continued to call for help at intervals; each shout was a mix of hope and fear. The effort it took to project my voice was immense, each cry leaving me more breathless than the last.

As the morning progressed, the hope that dawn had initially brought began to mingle with frustration.

Where was the help I so desperately needed?

Had God truly heard my pleas, or was this just another test of my resolve?

Yet, even in the face of this uncertainty, I couldn't give up. The daylight, for all its promises and shortcomings, had renewed my determination. If I could hold on a little longer, maybe, just maybe, someone would find me. The thought of rescue, returning to my family, and walking through the woods with Kelso by my side kept me fighting.

So there I lay, at the mercy of the elements and the passing of time, a man caught in a battle for survival. The morning light, with all its symbolic hope, had not yet brought relief, but it had reignited a flame within me, a refusal to surrender to despair. The story was far from over, each moment of light a reminder that even in our darkest hours, there is always a chance for a new dawn.

As the morning light grew stronger, a sound that once filled me with joy became a taunt— the distant hum of snowmobiles. These weren't the threatening roars of the night's winds or the eerie creaks of trees; these were signs of life, of people not far from where I lay trapped.

Yet, after a while and the first few times, their presence brought no relief, only a deeper despair. They rode by, one after the other, oblivious to my plight. Each passing engine was a reminder of how close help was, yet impossibly out of reach.

I called out, my voice barely more than a whisper against the roar of the engines, hoping by some miracle they would hear me. But they didn't stop; they never even slowed. The realization that I was invisible, hidden by the snow that entrapped me, was a bitter pill to swallow. I was so close to salvation, yet it might as well have been miles away.

My hope of being found and saved dwindled with each snowmobile that passed.

In those moments, my pleas to God took a darker turn. If this was to be my fate, left alone to the mercy of the cold and my injuries, then I wished for it to be over. The pain, the cold, and the repeated crashes of hope against the harsh rocks of reality had taken their toll. I was tired—tired of fighting, tired of hoping, tired of the relentless cycle of highs and lows. I wished for an end to the suffering, for the peace that I believed death would bring.

The irony of my situation wasn't lost on me. Here I was, a man who had dedicated his life to saving others, now unable to save himself. A man who had always been the one to respond to emergencies is now in desperate need of rescue. It was a humbling, heartbreaking realization that stripped away any illusions of control I thought I had over my life.

The solitude of my situation became more pronounced with each snowmobile that passed. The vibrant world of winter activities I had always loved was happening beyond my reach, a world I was no longer a part of. The stark contrast between my current state and those riders' freedom vividly reminds me how quickly life can change.

I lay there, face down in the snow, my thoughts a whirlwind of regret, fear, and fading hope. Once a place of adventure, the world around me was now indifferent to my suffering.

The sounds of the forest began to return as the morning progressed, the calls of birds and the rustling of small creatures in the snow, life continuing around me. Yet, these sounds, which would generally comfort me, now felt like a mockery of my predicament. I was a part of this world, yet apart from it, caught in a liminal space between life and death.

As time passed, my thoughts returned to my family, my children, and Kelso. Despite my pleas for an end, the love I held for them, the memories we shared, and the future I hoped to see kept flickering in the back of my mind. It was a cruel tug-of-war; the desire for relief from my suffering pitted against the longing to return to those I loved.

And so, as the morning unfolded, I remained there, a silent witness to the world moving on without me. My situation was unchanged, my fate still uncertain; I lay waiting for a miracle, for rescue, for any sign that I would not be left to face the cold embrace of death alone in the snow. The story of my fight for survival, for a chance to return to those I held dear, was still being written, each passing moment a testament to the will to live that burned within me, however faintly.

As the hours stretched on, a profound numbness took hold of me. The intense cold, fluctuating between -5 to -10 degrees throughout the night, had rendered me unable to feel any part of my body. Lying there in the woods, now somewhere over 12 hours since the crash, the absence of feeling was a small mercy in a situation where comfort was scarce.

Hour by hour, the realization that I was still here, still clinging to life despite the odds, became a beacon in the overwhelming darkness. Pain, a constant companion since the crash, had faded, dulled by the freezing temperatures that enveloped me.

My body temperature had plummeted, dangerously close to the threshold of unconsciousness. This critical detail, a stark indicator of my perilous situation, was a grim reminder of how close I teetered on the edge of survival. The morning brought activity, the buzz of engines, and voices in the distance, yet none of it reached the small patch of snow that had become my prison.

The reality of my continued isolation now tempered the hope that had flickered to life with the dawn's light. Each snowmobile that passed without a sign of noticing me was a blow to my already fragile hope. Yet, surrender was not an option. The instinct to survive, to hold on for a bit longer, refused to be extinguished.

In the silence between the passing machines, I reflected on the surreal nature of my predicament. The world around me, alive with the day's activities, was oblivious to the drama unfolding just off the beaten path. I was a ghost in my life, a spectator to a world moving on without me.

The struggle for survival had stripped everything down to its most basic elements: breath, warmth, visibility. These elements took on a significance I had never appreciated before. Each breath was a victory, each moment of retained warmth a gift, and the desire to be seen and found was a driving force.

Lying there, face down in the snow, the boundary between holding on and letting go became blurred in this liminal space, where life hung in the balance. Yet, even as my physical strength waned, the resolve to survive, to witness another day, to return to those I loved, burned with a quiet intensity.

As the chapter of this ordeal continued, with no end in sight, the journey became one of endurance, of reaching deep into the reserves of spirit and willpower I wasn't aware I possessed.

Chapter 8: The Glove

After what seemed like an eternity of daylight, a small miracle unfolded. A snowmobile finally stopped, just like the many that had passed obliviously. The wave of emotions that crashed over me was indescribable.

Relief, disbelief, gratitude—all these feelings and more swirled within me, creating a storm of overwhelming sensation. For what I assumed to be over 12 hours, I had been trapped, oscillating between hope and despair, fighting against the numbing cold and the creeping shadows of doubt. And now, finally, there was hope.

Even as the sound of the stopping snowmobile pierced through the silence, a part of me hesitated to embrace the full surge of hope that threatened to rise within. Was I hallucinating? After the long, harrowing hours that followed dawn, where each passing moment seemed to carry the potential for rescue only to leave me still stranded, I had learned to temper my expectations.

The rollercoaster of hope and disappointment had taken its toll, leaving me wary of letting my guard down too soon. The fear of once again facing unfilled hopes loomed large, a shadow cast over the flickering light of optimism that the sound of the snowmobile might have ignited.

In those moments, as I lay waiting, caught between the hope of rescue and the dread of another false alarm, my thoughts were a tangle of emotions. The desire to be found, pulled from the grasp of the cold and pain, warred with the instinct to protect myself from further disappointment. It was a delicate balance.

The sound of the snowmobile engine shutting off and the crunch of boots on snow as someone approached were signals I had longed for, yet part of me remained braced for the possibility that it might not lead to the rescue or that I may not survive the whole ordeal. This self-preservation tactic, born from hours of waiting and wondering, was a shield against the hurt that unmet expectations could bring.

Despite this caution, the human part of me, the part that yearned for connection, for rescue, couldn't help but lean into the hope that this time might be different. Each movement, each sound drawing nearer, stoked the embers of hope that had refused to be completely extinguished, even in the darkest moments.

The waiting, the listening for signs of rescue, became moments filled with a complex mix of dread and anticipation.

In those dawn hours, I did everything possible to keep my spirits up. Talking to myself had become my way of keeping the silence at bay, of reminding myself that I was still alive, still fighting. I'd even resorted to singing some songs, their melodies a balm to the frigid air and my fading spirits. It was about more than just passing the time; it was about maintaining that sliver of hope that someone would eventually find me.

The disbelief that someone had finally stopped was like a shock to my system. It took a moment for it to truly register for me to believe that this wasn't just another trick of my imagination, a cruel figment of hope. But then, the reality set in—rescue was at hand. I was going to make it. This thought and realization filled me with a surge of energy I hadn't felt in hours. Despite my injuries, despite the cold that had seeped into my very bones, I found a renewed strength and the human will to survive.

I stayed positive, clinging to the hope that had been reignited. Maintaining that optimism was a delicate balance, especially after such a long ordeal. But now, with the prospect of rescue within reach, it was as if a weight had been lifted. I talked to myself, offering encouragement and reassurance that I would be okay and that help had arrived.

As I lay there, waiting for the rescuer to reach me, I couldn't help but reflect on the journey that had brought me to this point. The fear, pain, and moments of despair were all part of this story, but so were the strength, hope, and sheer determination to hold on.

The person who had stopped, a stranger to me, was about to become a crucial part of my story, a hero in their own right. The gratitude I felt toward them was immense, a lifeline thrown to me in my moment of greatest need. Their voice calling out as they approached was the sweetest sound I had ever heard. It was the sound of a second chance.

The morning after the crash painted a scene of quiet desolation around me, the pristine snow untouched except for the dark, incongruous speck of my glove lying beside the trail. Yes, a glove. My right glove had somehow come off during the crash and was lying beside the trail. That glove, a mundane piece of my winter gear, became the beacon that ultimately saved my life. It lay there, a silent witness to the turmoil just off the path, a clue for the keen eyes that would find me.

The man who found me, whom I'd come to think of as my guardian angel, was drawn to that glove. It was a simple curiosity, the sight of something out of place against the white canvas of the snow, that prompted him to stop and investigate. Little did he know that his decision to veer off the beaten path would become the lifeline I desperately needed.

Lying there, I could barely make out his figure through my blurred and frostbitten vision. His voice, though, was clear and steady, comforting in the chaos of my mind. He kept talking to me, reassuring me that help was on the way and that I would be okay. His voice was the most beautiful sound in those moments, a harbinger of hope amidst the pain and fear.

Despite the gravity of my injuries, his arrival marked a turning point. The despair and loneliness enveloped me had begun to recede, replaced by a cautious optimism. For the first time in what felt like forever, I dared to believe that I might survive this ordeal, see my family again, feel the warmth of a fire, and hear the laughter of my children.

The arrival of Ron, the man who would become my unforeseen savior, felt nothing short of miraculous. The scene of our encounter, marked by the solitary glove that caught his eye, was the peculiarities that fate can throw our way. He was riding that day in a group of eight snowmobiles. He was the second to last in line heading north on the trail. He saw my glove that came off during the crash and thought it didn't look right. So, he turned around on the trail.

Ron, with his quick wit and keen observation, quipped, "No one loses just one glove and keeps on snowmobiling!"

His simple yet profound words cut through the tension like a knife.

Despite the gravity of the situation, I couldn't help but laugh—a sound so foreign and yet so welcome in that moment of relief. A peal of laughter carried with it the weight of survived danger, a brief respite from the ordeal that had been my reality for over half a day.

The absurdity of the glove, lying on the snow's edge as a silent beacon of my plight, was not lost. I have always wondered, when I see a lone shoe on the side of the highway, who loses one shoe? An oddity that sparks curiosity and wonder. This comparison, humorous in its truth, was a reminder of how the most mundane objects can become symbols of something far greater in extraordinary circumstances.

My attire, the snowmobiling gear produced by the Yamaha Corporation, from the bibs to the boots, played no small part in my survival. You may wonder why I was wearing Yamaha gear while riding an Arctic Cat. Simple, I got a great deal on it. The quality of this gear, designed to withstand the rigors of winter sports, undoubtedly played a pivotal role in keeping the worst of the cold at bay. In a situation where every degree of warmth counted, the insulation and protection it offered might have been the difference between life and death.

Ron's observations and actions underscored a fundamental truth about human nature: the instinct to help, connect, and bring humor into even the most dire situations. His decision to stop, prompted by nothing more than a lone glove in the snow, set the chain of events that led to my rescue.

Gratitude, relief, and a renewed belief in the possibility of miracles swelled within me, pushing against the boundaries of what I thought was possible. The ordeal stretched my faith to its limits, both in myself and in the possibility of divine intervention. Yet, here I was, witnessing what felt like a miracle unfold before my eyes.

My heart was so full it seemed to expand beyond my chest, and though my eyes struggled to stay open, weary from the strain and stress, I was acutely aware of everything happening around me.

Ron's arrival was more than just a physical rescue; it restored faith. Faith in humanity, the kindness of strangers, and the notion that even in our darkest hours, there can be light.

The gratitude I felt towards him, towards everyone who would play a part in my rescue, was immense. It was a deep, profound thankfulness that words could scarcely capture. This man, who had been a stranger until now, had chosen to stop to investigate a lone glove in the snow and, in doing so, had become my lifeline.

John, a man riding in Ron's group, dialed 911. The reality of being found started to settle in, wrapping around me like a warm blanket against the biting cold. The moment he made the call, it felt like a heavy weight was being lifted from my shoulders, a burden I had carried through the longest hours of my life. With the push of a button, Ron and John turned into my much-awaited cavalry.

As we waited for the rescue team to arrive, the happiness and relief filled me and gave me peace. Despite the pain, the cold, and the fear that had been constant companions, there was a sense of being exactly where I was meant to be at that moment. The belief in humanity, which had flickered and waned throughout the night, was now rekindled, burning brightly within me.

The rescue was a blur of motion and emotion when it finally happened. Each movement was agonizing yet filled with an incredible sense of relief. As I was carefully extracted from my snowy entrapment and tended to, the reality of my situation began to sink in. I had survived. Against the odds, I had held on through the coldest night. The longest night of my life. And now I was being given the opportunity to live on.

The wait for the emergency services felt both agonizingly slow and startlingly quick. Time, which had stretched and contracted strangely throughout my ordeal, now seemed to race forward. Each minute passed was a step closer to safety, warmth, and life beyond the snow and trees that had been my prison. Another rider in Ron's party was an EMT named Sarah. I thought, wow, what are the chances of that! Sarah got to work assessing my injuries and reassuring me I was no longer alone.

The belief in miracles, in the intervention of a higher power, had been an abstract concept. Now, they were as real as the snow that blanketed the ground. My pleas, my prayers, had been answered in the most unexpected ways, reaffirming my faith in the unseen and the power of hope and prayer.

Chapter 9: My First Helicopter Ride

As the reality of rescue sank in with John's 911 call, a flurry of activity soon unfolded around me, though I could see none. My senses were focused on the sounds and sensations as the rescue team arrived, a group of first responders whose presence signaled that the worst was truly over. I could hear the crunch of boots on snow and the soft murmuring of voices coordinating their efforts to get to me. The sound of each voice and each step they took in the snow built a picture of hope and action in my mind.

As I remember, the first person to reach me was a woman EMT whose voice cut through the cold with a calm, assertive kindness that immediately put me at ease. She inquired about my injuries with professional concern, and her questions were clear and methodical.

As she spoke, I felt the gentle but firm touch of hand warmer packets being tucked around my neck and back, an attempt to chase away the deep chill that had settled into my bones. The warmth they provided was a small comfort but a profound one, hinting at the return to a world where pain wasn't the dominant sensation.

Soon, the surrounding area buzzed with more rescuers, their movements orchestrated to secure my safety. The sound of a saw cutting through the branches that ensnared my leg filled the air, a careful symphony of rescue efforts that underscored the seriousness of my situation. Despite the intensity of their task, the team's efficiency and gentle handling made it clear I was in the hands of skilled professionals.

When it was time to move me onto a longboard for transport, the complexity of the task became apparent. Positioned carefully beside me, the board was a bridge back to safety. The process of being turned over onto it was a blur of motions and commands, my body responding only faintly to the manipulation due to the numbness that pervaded it. I couldn't see the faces of those who helped me, but their steady, reassuring presence was palpable. I felt hands guiding my arms and legs, which seemed to have a will of their own, slipping off the board in a display of my body's betrayal by the cold and injuries.

The rescuers worked with an effort to lift me, their count-off to heave resonating with urgency and care. It took multiple attempts, with the team adjusting their grips and reaffirming their positions, their voices a mix of professional calm and human concern. Finally, securely on the longboard, I was lifted wholly, carried by what seemed like an army of unseen angels whose faces I could only imagine.

As they transported me onto the main trail, the motion was smooth, and each step was measured to avoid pushing around. The voices of the rescuers melded into a backdrop of relief, each word and action wrapping around me like a blanket, insulating me from the fear that had gripped me for so long. I was moving, really moving towards safety, each movement away from the place of my confinement a step towards recovery and life.

As the rescuers secured me onto the longboard, their next step was transferring me onto a UTV cot specifically designed for such rescues. This transfer was yet another testament to their skill and coordination. I felt the motion as they lifted me, the sensation of moving through the air briefly before being gently placed down again. Each movement was precise, and the care they took was precise in the steadiness of their actions.

My helmet and goggles still obscured my vision, rendering me unable to see the faces of those who were working so diligently to save me. This blindness added an extra layer of reliance and trust; I was completely in the hands of these professionals, trusting them not just to manage my physical well-being but also to guide me out of the wilderness that had almost claimed my life.

The ride on the UTV was a surreal experience. I could feel the vibrations and hear the engine's rumble as we moved along the trail, each turn and bump a reminder of the rugged terrain that had been my adventure playground and perilous trap. Though relatively short, the journey felt extended, as if each minute was dense with the raw reality of survival and rescue.

Once we reached the ambulance, the atmosphere shifted from urgent field rescue to meticulous medical assessment. The space inside the ambulance felt simultaneously confining and comforting, a sanctuary where the next phase of my ordeal would unfold.

Here, the medical team began their thorough evaluation, checking my injuries with clinical precision yet compassionate care. The sound of medical equipment, the soft voices discussing my condition, and the occasional touch as they assessed my injuries created a buzz of activity around me, and each action was aimed at stabilizing my condition.

My inability to see did not hinder my connection with each rescuer and medical professional throughout this process. Their voices were kind and reassuring, giving me a picture through words and explaining what was happening and what to expect next. This verbal communication was crucial for my understanding and maintaining that trust thread that had been vital since Ron first found me.

As they detailed their findings and planned their next steps, the reality of my situation continued to sink in. I was no longer alone in the forest; I was on my way to receiving the medical attention I desperately needed. The transition from the raw, elemental fight for survival in the snow to an ambulance's clinical, controlled environment marked a significant shift in my journey from peril to safety.

As the ambulance sped toward the designated meeting point for the flight for life helicopter, the activity inside the vehicle intensified. The EMTs, two women whose voices were both stern yet comforting, explained that they needed to cut off my snowmobile gear to assess and treat my injuries properly.

Despite my protests—those clothes were my favorite and represented many memories of adventures past—I was in no position to argue effectively. I bargained and pleaded. I said, "Just slide them off! I can't feel anything anyway!" My plea to keep the clothing intact was met with gentle laughter and sympathetic yet firm reassurances as they carefully removed each layer, slicing through the fabric with clinical precision.

Though necessary, the loss of my gear felt like another small defeat in a night full of challenges. For me, it was more than just fabric being cut away; it felt like they were slicing through the last vestiges of my normalcy, the adventure-seeking part of me that had donned that gear with anticipation of a thrilling ride. Now, here I was, unable to feel the cold that the gear was designed to protect against, feeling vulnerable and exposed both physically and emotionally.

The hypothermia I was experiencing muddled my thoughts, making it hard to process everything that was happening with the clarity I once took for granted. My brain seemed to lag, catching up slowly with the reality around me.

The EMTs continued to talk to me, their voices a steady stream of reassurance that pierced through the fog of confusion. They told me I would make it, and their words were designed to comfort but also anchor me to the present, to keep me engaged and fighting.

As we arrived at the local casino parking lot, which had been cleared to serve as a makeshift helipad, I was transferred from the ambulance to the care of the flight crew. Two flight nurses stepped into the ambulance and took over from the EMTs, receiving a detailed report of my condition and reassuring me just as fervently that I was in good hands.

The environment shifted from the relative stability of the ambulance to the charged atmosphere of emergency flight care. Despite being unable to see anything—my vision still obscured by my helmet and goggles—I could sense the urgency and precision in their movements. Their confident and professional voices filled the space, outlining their steps and explaining their actions as they prepared me for the flight.

Being in that ambulance, surrounded by medical professionals all working diligently to save my life, brought back memories of my own time as a firefighter and EMT. I remembered being the one giving reassurances, the one telling patients that they would be okay. On the other side, I understood more profoundly the weight of those reassurances, the hope they were meant to instill.

The surreal feeling of being cared for, of being the patient after years of being the caregiver, added a layer of surrealism to the experience. I was mentally alert, trapped in a body that no longer responded as it should, reliant on the expertise and kindness of others. As the flight nurses finalized preparations for transport, their efficient care and calm demeanor provided some comfort. I was reminded that despite the chaos of the situation, I was not alone—I was in capable hands, surrounded by a team of professionals whose sole focus was my well-being.

The transition from the ambulance to the flight for life helicopter marked my first-ever helicopter ride—an experience under circumstances far removed from anything I could have imagined. The space felt incredibly confined as the flight crew maneuvered me into the helicopter. I could sense the tight fit, with my feet brushing against the sides of the aircraft. This sensation came not from pain or discomfort, which were numbed by my condition, but merely from the contact, a stark reminder of how closely confined I was in this flying lifeline.

As we lifted off, the flight nurses continued to monitor my condition, their presence a constant in the cramped quarters of the helicopter. They informed me we were headed to Aspirus Hospital in Wausau, Wisconsin, the closest medical facility equipped to handle severe trauma cases like mine. The reality of being airborne in a rescue helicopter, unable to see my surroundings but acutely aware of every movement, was surreal. The hum of the rotor blades created a continuous backdrop of noise, adding to the intensity of the experience.

Throughout the flight, the nurses kept up a steady stream of communication. They checked my vitals, administered necessary medical care, and reassured me about the process. Their professionalism helped to anchor me, providing a sense of security amidst the whirlwind of sensations and the underlying fear of the unknown. Their explanations and updates on our progress to the hospital were crucial in keeping me informed, helping to ground me in reality as we made our way through the air.

Despite the critical nature of my condition, the flight was smooth. The pilot's expertise and the medical team's coordinated efforts ensured that every aspect of the transport was optimized for speed and safety. Every inch of space was utilized inside the helicopter, with medical equipment and personnel fitting tightly around me. The cramped space underscored the seriousness of the situation, with every piece of gear and every flight crew action focused on stabilizing my condition until we could reach the hospital.

During this ride to the hospital, I realized I couldn't see anything outside because I still had my helmet on strapped down to the longboard. Trying to lighten the mood, I joked to one of the flight nurses, "Hey, I can't see out the window!"

At first, he looked confused, but then he got the joke and started laughing. It felt good to make someone laugh, even in such a serious situation. Somewhere inside my head, I knew this was my first helicopter ride, and I was at a loss for words about missing out on the view from above.

He laughed briefly and then reassured me, "You're going to be fine."

His words, simple and straightforward, made me feel a bit better. It was a small moment, but it mattered. It reminded me that there were people taking care of me who could still smile and laugh even when things were intense.

That little joke and the nurse's laughter helped distract me from the pain and the worry. For a moment, it made the situation feel less overwhelming. It was nice to remember that there was still room for humor and human connection, even during this emergency.

The helicopter ride to the hospital lasted about 20 minutes. They gave me some strong pain medication during the flight, which might have made the time seem shorter than it was. The whole experience was a blur, partly because of the meds and partly because everything was happening so fast.

Once we landed, the medical team wasted no time. I was quickly moved from the helicopter to a stretcher and rushed into the trauma room of the emergency department. As soon as we entered the ER, various medical professionals surrounded me. They sprang into action immediately, working together smoothly and efficiently.

I was still wearing my helmet, so my view was blocked, but I could hear the urgent voices of doctors and nurses and the sounds of medical equipment being moved around. It was overwhelming but reassuring to hear the controlled urgency in their voices. They knew exactly what they were doing.

Finally, the ER doctor removed my helmet, and suddenly, I could see the faces of the people helping me. Lying there on the table, I felt exposed yet incredibly supported at the same time. The room was filled with medical staff; each person focused on their tasks, working quickly to assess my condition and start treatment.

Even though everything was still a bit blurry, and I was in and out of full awareness because of the medication and the shock, I could sense the competence and dedication of everyone in the room. It was clear that I was in very capable hands, giving me a deep sense of security despite the chaos around me. The professionalism and immediate care I received were remarkable, and I felt incredibly grateful to receive such expert attention.

When I arrived at the trauma room, one of the first things the doctors checked was my body temperature. It was shockingly low, just 86 degrees Fahrenheit. The doctor informed me of this with a serious tone, making it clear I understood how critical the situation was. My body needed to be warmed up before they could even consider taking me to surgery.

To help raise my temperature, the medical team used a device called a bear hugger. This machine works like a large, inflatable blanket that envelops the body. It has tubes that circulate warm liquid around and beneath you, gently and gradually heating your body to a safer temperature. Lying there, surrounded by the warmth of the bear hugger, I started to feel the chill in my bones recede.

As the warmth slowly seeped into my body, I felt a profound sense of relief. Despite the severity of my condition, the competence and quick actions of the medical staff around me reassured me. I knew I was in the best possible hands, and their attentive care made me believe that I was going to make it through this ordeal.

In the trauma room, wrapped in the technology and care designed to save lives, I felt a deep gratitude. Despite the pain and initial fear, the bear hugger's warmth stabilized my physical state and comforted me emotionally.

It was a moment of quiet in the storm of activity where I could finally believe I was truly on the path to recovery. Knowing that the staff were doing everything possible to ensure my survival, I felt a profound trust in their abilities and a newfound hope that I would live to see another day. A day that I had no hopes for just hours before the ordeal, lying face down in the snow.

Chapter 10: No Frostbite

As I lay in the trauma room, enveloped in the bear hugger's warmth, I was acutely aware of the odd sensation—or lack thereof—in my limbs. Throughout the ordeal, my arms and legs had become completely numb, a state that had paradoxically been both a curse and a blessing. The numbness descended gradually, like the slow fading of light at dusk, until I was left without any feeling in them. It was as if they weren't even part of my body anymore.

This peculiar sensation was unsettling, yet I understood it was crucial to my survival through the night. Normally, such a lack of sensation would be alarming, a clear signal of something dire. But the harsh conditions I faced shielded me from what would have otherwise been unbearable pain.

It's difficult to describe the feeling accurately—it's like when your limbs fall asleep, but imagine that feeling deepening to the point where you feel absolutely nothing. No cold, no pain - nothing. It's as though they weren't there at all.

In those moments, lying in the hospital and slowly regaining warmth, I began to test the presence of my limbs by trying to move them slightly. It was a surreal experience when you couldn't feel them respond. The medical team monitored this carefully, explaining that while the numbness had protected me from pain, it was also a sign of how critical my condition was. The blood circulation to my limbs had been severely compromised, and there was a real risk of long-term damage.

As the Bear Hugger did its work, raising my body temperature to a safer level, I reflected on the events of the past hours. It was almost surreal to think about how close I had come to a fatal outcome, only to be pulled back from the brink by small miracles and professional excellence. The warmth from the device was like a physical manifestation of all the good fortune I had experienced—each degree it raised my temperature felt like another step away from danger.

This period of waiting, wrapped in the Bear Hugger, was also a time of introspection. I pondered the random chance that had led to my rescue—the glove on the trail, Ron's timely arrival, the expertise of the ambulance crew and the flight team, and the care in the hospital. It seemed like a series of coincidences, but part of me felt there was something more, perhaps a guiding hand or a fate that had plans for me beyond that snowy trail.

I also thought about the people who had helped me—how each of them had a role that was crucial in the chain of survival that had ensnared me from death's grip. There was a kind of orchestrated grace to it all, from the emergency response on the snowy trail to the high-tech treatment in the hospital. This experience reaffirmed my faith in human capability and compassion and in some greater force that seemed to be looking out for me.

When I was warm enough for surgery, I felt a strange sense of peace. The anxiety and stress gave way to a steadfast readiness to face whatever came next. I trusted the hands I was in and that whatever happened, there was a reason I had made it this far. I was ready for surgery, ready to heal, and, most importantly, ready to continue whatever path lay ahead with a new appreciation for life and the many forces—both seen and unseen—that sustain it.

I could feel the faintest hints of sensation returning. It started as a tingling, much like the prickling of pins and needles, but even that slight sensation was a sign of recovery, a message from my body that it was fighting to heal. The medical team was attentive, adjusting the bear hugger and assessing the returning blood flow, and their professionalism and care never wavered.

Their reassurances that the numbness was expected under the circumstances and their explanations of how they planned to address it provided immense comfort. They outlined their strategies for minimizing potential damage and discussed the treatments they would use to stimulate circulation and nerve response.

Each small movement, each faint feeling that began to return to my limbs, was a victory. Even though these sensations were minimal and sometimes uncomfortable, they proved that recovery was possible. The team's meticulous care and the technology enveloping me were slowly coaxing my body back from the edge it had teetered on just hours before.

During this time, my thoughts often drifted to my current state and the solitary helplessness I felt while lying in the snow. Now, surrounded by experts and advanced medical equipment, the fear of permanent loss began to recede. Instead, a feeling of hope took root that recovery was within reach. I believed that with time and the right medical support, I might regain full function.

Remarkably, despite my severe conditions, I emerged without frostbite. Yes! This was even more astonishing, considering I had lost one of my gloves during the crash. During that frigid night, when temperatures dipped to -10°F, my hand was exposed directly to the snow. It's a fact that still baffles me and everyone else who hears about the ordeal. Logically, it seems impossible; medically, it's almost a miracle.

The lack of frostbite, especially on my exposed hand, is something for which I credit the high-quality snowmobiling gear I was wearing, designed explicitly by the Yamaha company. This clothing was engineered for extreme conditions and intended to keep snowmobilers safe and warm in environments just like the one I found myself in. The materials used likely shielded me from the worst of the cold, maintaining enough body heat to prevent frostbite despite the prolonged exposure.

Looking back, it's hard to fully grasp how I survived that night without more severe consequences. Circumstances were against me: the cold, my injuries, the isolation. Yet, here I was, in a hospital bed, relatively intact. This outcome, I believe, was not just a stroke of luck but also a testament to the effectiveness of my gear. The technology embedded in that snowmobiling suit must have played a critical role in insulating me and preserving my core temperature at a crucial time.

In those moments of reflection, I felt an overwhelming sense of gratitude towards the designers and manufacturers of that gear. The foresight to create clothing capable of withstanding such harsh conditions undoubtedly saved my life.

It's fascinating to think that the decisions made by textile engineers, whom I've never met, profoundly impacted my survival. It underscored how seemingly small choices, like what gear to wear on a snowmobiling trip, can have life-altering implications.

The hospital staff, too, were amazed by my condition, given the circumstances. Their assessments and continuous monitoring were meticulous, checking over and over for any signs of frostbite or deeper cold-related injuries. Each new confirmation that no frost damage added to the sense of miracle surrounding my survival story.

As I lay there being treated, these thoughts circled through my mind, mingling with the physical sensations of thawing and the emotional relief of being safe. It was a lot to process: the shock of the accident, the ordeal of the night, the sudden rescue, and the slow realization of how close I had come to a very different outcome.

This experience gave me a profound respect for the resilience of the human body and spirit. Lying in that hospital bed, slowly warming, feeling the tingles of returning sensation in my limbs, I knew I had been given a second chance. The gratitude I felt for my rescuers, the medical team, and even the designers of my snowmobiling suit was immense and indescribable.

I also realized that this event was a pivotal point in my life. Not only had I survived a night that could easily have claimed my life, but I had also gained new insights into the value of preparation, the advances in emergency medical response, and the sheer unpredictability of life. Each of these realizations shaped my thoughts and actions long after my recovery was complete.

As I recovered in the hospital, these thoughts often occupied my mind. They mingled with the gratitude given to my rescuers and medical team, blending into a profound appreciation for all the elements that contributed to my survival. Each component—from the physical gear to the skilled hands of those who saved me—formed a link in the chain of survival that brought me back from the edge.

This ordeal also instilled in me a passion to advocate for safety and preparedness in all outdoor sports. Sharing my story isn't just about recounting a personal experience; it's about highlighting the undeniable value of proper equipment and preparation. It's a call to all who enjoy the wild spaces of our world to not only respect nature's power but equip themselves against its unpredictability.

Getting back to the hospital part, I entered the trauma room at Aspirus in the late morning of February 24th, 2022, which marked a critical phase in my ordeal. After enduring a night of unimaginable hardship, this was the moment where the extent of my physical injuries would be thoroughly assessed and treated. The trauma room, a hub of medical activity, was where the hospital's capabilities were fully directed toward saving lives and mitigating severe injuries.

As I was wheeled in, the immediate shift from the cold, uncertain environment of the outdoors to the controlled chaos of the emergency room was relieving. The trauma team was ready and waiting, a group of professionals, each skilled in their respective roles, from surgeons to nurses, all prepared for whatever challenge I brought through their doors.

Despite the severity of my situation, the atmosphere in the room was one of calm efficiency. The team moved with purpose, their actions swift but deliberate. Clearly, this was a routine for them, yet each movement and decision carried the weight of critical importance. The way they handled my case with professionalism and care was nothing short of what I would describe as medical *'magic.'*

They began by conducting a thorough assessment of my injuries. This involved a series of X-rays and scans to determine the extent of my fractures and internal injuries. As they worked, they communicated with each other in concise, clear terms, ensuring every detail was noted and every possibility considered. The focus was intense, yet there was a sense of compassion in their interactions with me.

I was mostly silent, still processing the fact that I was finally safe, yet the emotional impact of my experience was deep. Feeling the gentle hands of the medical staff as they examined and treated my injuries, I was overwhelmed with gratitude. Each stitch, each bandage applied, felt like a step away from the brink of death I had teetered on just hours before.

The seriousness of my injuries required multiple interventions. My right arm had both lower bones broken in compound fractures, my left elbow was dislocated and broken, my left leg had a mid-femur compound fracture, and the knee was broken at the tibial plateau, and my right leg had a torn MCL and ACL. These broken bones needed to be set and immobilized. The wounds needed to be cleaned and dressed. Pain management was a priority as the numbness wore off, and the reality of my injuries manifested in intense discomfort. The staff administered medications to ease the pain, always explaining their actions and ensuring I understood what was happening and why.

Throughout this process, the team's demeanor was incredibly reassuring. Despite their focus on the medical tasks at hand, they made sure to maintain a human connection with me. They asked me how I felt, offered encouragement, and even shared light-hearted comments to ease the tension. Their ability to blend professionalism with empathy was remarkable and significantly impacted my ability to cope with the situation.

As I lay there, being patched up and ready for surgery, I couldn't help but reflect on the journey that had led me to this point. From the initial crash in the wilderness to the moment I was found and now lying in a hospital bed, it was a trajectory filled with pain but also incredible human kindness and professional dedication.

The team at Aspirus Hospital did not just treat my physical injuries; they also helped to restore my spirit. Their tireless efforts stabilized my condition but reaffirmed my faith in the good that healthcare professionals do every day. It was a profound reminder of the importance of emergency medical services and their impact on lives.

As the hours passed and the initial treatments were completed, I was moved from the trauma room to the surgery room, where I spent somewhere close to 13 hours, and then off to the ICU after that. The relief that came with knowing the worst was over was immense. I was alive, in recovery, and the best hands possible. The gratitude I felt toward everyone who had a part in saving my life was overwhelming. Each person contributed to a chain of survival that had brought me back from the edge, a journey of pain, hope, and, ultimately, survival.

Despite the pain and the haze of medications, I was acutely aware of how fortunate I was. The situation could have ended much differently had it not been for my rescuers' quick actions, the medical staff's expertise, and the divine intervention that was with me that night. There was a profound sense of relief knowing that I was no longer alone against the elements but instead surrounded by professionals equipped to save my life.

Chapter 11: Treatment Phase

As I moved into the next phase of my medical ordeal, the gravity of the situation continued to unfold. After being stabilized in the trauma room, it was clear that the road to recovery was going to be a long and challenging one.

In the trauma room, the medical team had to employ a King line IV, a large bore intravenous line inserted into my neck. Given the extent of the injuries to my limbs, traditional IV sites were not viable. This was just one of the many complications they had to navigate due to the severe nature of my injuries. The placement of the King line was crucial for administering the necessary fluids and medications to stabilize my condition during the surgery.

The surgery itself was extensive and complex. During this time, surgeons worked meticulously to repair the numerous injuries I had sustained. Every broken bone and every internal issue that they had identified in the trauma room needed attention. It was a testament to their skill and determination that they addressed each issue in one continuous, grueling session.

I have no memory of the surgery itself. The combination of heavy anesthesia and the sheer trauma of my experience left me with no recollection of that night or much of the following day. It was a blank in my life, hours lost to the haze of recovery and medication. The first few memories I have post-surgery are fragmented, my brain slowly piecing everything together as I regained consciousness over the next couple of days in the hospital's intensive care unit.

The environment of the ICU was a stark contrast to the chaos of the trauma room. Here, everything was measured with a steady rhythm dictated by the beeps of monitors and the periodic checks by nurses and doctors. Each visit from the medical staff brought a little more information about what had been done during surgery and what my recovery process would entail. I was informed of how much Titanium was now inside my body. My right forearm was rebuilt using plates and screws from this incredible metal. My left leg had a rod of Titanium pounded up from the knee area to complete my femur once again.

Despite the pain and the slow fog of recovery, there was an underlying sense of relief. Each update from the doctors, every slight improvement in my condition, felt like a victory. I was alive, and with each passing hour, my body was mending. The complexity of the surgeries and the careful monitoring highlighted just how precarious my situation had been and how much skill and effort was being put into ensuring my recovery.

This period in the ICU was not just about physical healing but also about mental and emotional recovery. Being surrounded by caring professionals who managed my physical needs and addressed my fears and concerns was invaluable. They provided reassurance, detailed explanations of my progress, and constant encouragement, which were as crucial to my recovery as the surgical interventions.

As days passed, the fragments of my memory began to knit together, forming a clearer picture of the ordeal I had survived and the path ahead. The hospital became a world unto itself, where each step forward was measured, and each small improvement was celebrated.

As I began to regain a clearer sense of awareness in the ICU, the enormity of what I had just endured started to sink in truly. Realizing that I had survived an entire night in the harsh wilderness under extreme conditions was miraculous. It wasn't just me who felt this way; the hospital staff shared the sentiment. Word of my survival and dramatic rescue had spread throughout the hospital, and it seemed to stir a mixture of awe and curiosity among the staff.

In those days following the surgery, my hospital room slowly turned into a gathering place. Nurses, doctors, and other hospital employees would often stop by for medical checks and sometimes to see the man who had beaten the odds so dramatically. Each visit often starts with a medical purpose but then shifts toward a more personal interaction.

"Can't believe you're the one we've all been hearing about," a nurse might say, her tone a mix of professional respect and genuine wonder.

These interactions, while brief, brought a different energy into my recovery space. They were reminders of the unusual nature of my case, which seemed to provide a break from the routine hospital environment, not just for me but also for the staff.

Some staff would ask permission to sit with me for a few minutes, eager to hear parts of my story directly from me. As I shared, I saw their expressions shift from professional detachment to deep human connection. These moments were therapeutic, not just for my physical recovery, but they also helped me process the emotional and psychological impact of the ordeal.

I was dubbed the "patient celebrity" in a lighthearted way, which was surreal. This nickname was tossed around with smiles in the hallways and even during handoffs between shifts. While it was odd at first to be known for such a harrowing experience, I soon realized that this interest wasn't about the sensationalism of my survival story.

Rather, it was about the affirmation of life and their professional pride in seeing someone recover from such extreme circumstances. It was clear that my story had touched a chord with many, perhaps as a reminder of why they had chosen their professions in the first place—to save lives and witness the strength of the human spirit.

These interactions also illuminated the less visible aspects of healthcare—the emotional support and the shared human experiences that are vital in the healing process. Each person who entered my room left a mark on my recovery, providing encouragement and often sharing a bit of their own lives in return. This exchange of stories and support was an unexpected and valuable aspect of my time in the ICU.

After my initial recovery in the ICU, where the immediate and most life-threatening injuries were addressed, I was moved to the trauma floor. This transition marked a new phase in my lengthy hospital stay. It was a step forward, away from the constant, intense monitoring of the ICU, to a place where the focus shifted more toward long-term recovery and rehabilitation.

Over the next 25 days or so, my medical journey involved a series of surgeries that were aimed at repairing the extensive damage my body had endured. Each procedure was targeted at different injuries, each with its complexities and challenges.

One of the more significant surgeries was on my right forearm. During my ordeal in the wilderness, I sustained severe compound fractures, and the initial surgery involved installing titanium plates to stabilize both bones. However, the trauma was so extensive that the swelling in my arm was massive. It reached a point where the surgeon was unable to close the incision properly.

As a result, I had to be fitted with a wound vacuum, commonly known as a wound vac. This device is crucial in situations like mine; it continuously applies negative pressure to draw out fluid from the wound, which helps reduce swelling and promotes healing.

The wound vac was an odd sensation, to say the least. It was another machine tethered to my body, yet it was a critical step toward healing. I spent weeks with this machine attached to my arm – the feeling of a constant, gentle suction on this part of my arm became a part of my daily existence in the hospital.

After several weeks with the wound vac, my arm's swelling had reduced sufficiently for the surgeon to attempt closing the wound again. This was not a simple procedure—it took a couple of attempts, reflecting the delicate balance the medical team had to maintain between fostering healing and not rushing the process, which could lead to complications.

During this time, the trauma floor became a familiar place for me. I became accustomed to the staff there, and their visits have become a part of my daily routine. Yet, each nurse, doctor, and therapist played a specific role in my recovery. Their professionalism and care were evident in their medical expertise and in the encouragement they offered during an incredibly tough time for me.

The pain management was a critical component of my recovery. Post-surgery pain is intense, and managing it is crucial not just for comfort but also to enable physical therapy and rehabilitation exercises. The pain management team worked closely with my surgeons and nurses to adjust my medications, ensuring that I received relief while avoiding any complications.

Physical therapists also began working with me during this period. The surgeries saved my limbs and stabilized my injuries, but the real work of regaining strength and functionality was beginning. The physiotherapy sessions were exhausting and painful but necessary. Each tiny movement was a victory, each step an achievement.

During the first two and a half weeks of my hospital stay, I found myself in a vulnerable state. Following the series of surgeries required to stabilize my fractures and to address internal injuries, I was left with no functional use of my arms or legs. This immobility presented not just a physical challenge but also an emotional and psychological battle.

Lying in my hospital bed, day and night, unable to move or care for myself, I depended entirely on the hospital staff. The reality of my situation was stark—I was completely reliant on others for even the most basic needs. This dependency extended to every aspect of my daily life, from personal hygiene to feeding.

The nursing staff, consisting of RNs and CNAs, showed incredible compassion and professionalism during this intense period. Each mealtime underscored my helplessness as they carefully fed me by hand. It was a humbling experience that deeply affected my perspective on life and the often-overlooked dignity in receiving care.

Despite the undoubtedly demanding nature of their work, not once did any staff member show frustration or impatience. Their demeanor was always one of understanding and support, providing physical assistance and emotional comfort.

A series of small yet significant interactions characterized this period. Each spoonful of food, each adjustment in the bed, and every routine check were carried out with a kindness that went beyond mere professional duty. These actions were affirmations of their commitment to my recovery and well-being.

The lack of mobility brought physical limitations and a deep sense of vulnerability. During these weeks, I truly understood the importance of compassionate care in healing. The staff's empathy and attentiveness helped alleviate the emotional burden of my condition, offering reassurance and encouragement during a time of great personal distress.

As days turned into weeks, the focus of my medical team gradually shifted from acute medical intervention to rehabilitation. Physical therapists began to visit more frequently, each session aimed at restoring some degree of independence. These sessions were grueling and painful, yet crucial for recovery. The therapists guided me through various exercises designed to rebuild strength and mobility, each movement a challenge against the stiffness and weakness that had set into my limbs.

The goal was clear: to regain enough function to perform basic tasks independently. While the progress was slow and often frustrating, the physical therapists' support and the nursing staff's continued care provided continuous motivation. Each small improvement, every slight movement I could execute independently, was celebrated as a milestone.

One of the more poignant moments in my recovery was learning how to feed myself again. By the third week, I could hold an elongated fork, a device designed to help patients with limited mobility eat more independently. Although I still couldn't bring the fork close to my mouth, mastering this tool was a significant step towards regaining some semblance of normalcy.

The pride I felt in these small victories was immense, bolstered by the constant support and encouragement of the hospital staff. They were not just caregivers but my cheerleaders, always there with a kind word or a moment to listen, keeping my spirits high even when it seemed impossible.

My physiotherapists were dedicated and relentless from the very start of my physical therapy. They began by simply moving my limbs for me as I lay immobile. I couldn't sit up on my own, barely able to close my hands or move my feet. But they persisted, gently pushing me each day to go a little further and to try a little harder. Their approach was always supportive, never forceful, yet they knew how to motivate me, even when I felt like giving up.

Three weeks into my hospital stay, physical therapy became a fundamental part of my daily routine. Therapists would come to my room every weekday to help me move and stretch, gradually coaxing my limbs back to life. The sessions were grueling yet vital, pushing me to regain the strength and mobility that seemed so distant in the aftermath of my surgeries.

The daily routine of physical therapy quickly became something I looked forward to. It marked progress, a tangible sign that I was moving forward, however slowly. Though exhausting, each session brought a sense of accomplishment and hope. The therapists' expertise and encouragement were crucial in helping me understand that each slight movement was a step toward recovery and leaving the hospital not in a wheelchair but on my own two feet.

By the fourth week of therapy, I reached a milestone that felt like a turning point in my recovery. With the help of my physical therapist, I attempted to stand up from my wheelchair. Using only my right leg, I managed to stand for about 30 seconds. Though it might seem brief, those 30 seconds were monumental for me. It made me very emotional. Standing up and feeling the weight on my leg, even for half a minute, made me feel more human than I had in a long time. It was a physical reassurance that recovery was possible and that I was regaining control over my body.

The hospital staff celebrated my successes with me, provided comfort during setbacks, and continuously reminded me of the progress I was making. As I continued to work with the physical therapy team, my days in the hospital began to feel less like a sentence and more like a journey toward recovery. Each session built on the last, and each movement brought me closer to independence. Each day ended with a stronger belief in my ability to recover.

The Aspirus Hospital sits in a location roughly an hour and a half drive from Green Bay. This distance meant that any visit from friends and family wasn't just a casual drop-in; it required a commitment of time and braving the often treacherous winter roads. Despite these challenges, my friend, Brian, who lived in the Green Bay area, made the long journey to see me numerous times. He visited at least twice a week, underscoring the depth of our friendship and his support during this incredibly tough time.

Brian's visits were a lifeline for me. Each time he walked through the door, he would bring me something as simple as a Diet Coke or a sub, and it was as though a piece of my normal life was restored, even if just for a short while. His presence brought comfort and a connection to the world outside the hospital walls—a world that seemed so distant yet desperately needed. Despite the distance and the harsh winter conditions, his efforts to be there meant more than he probably realized. It was a powerful reminder of the strength of human connections and the lengths we go to support the people important to us.

The feeling of isolation at Aspirus was eating me. Being so far from home made the hospital seem like a place out of time and space, especially as the weeks turned into a month. I completely missed the transition from winter to spring, locked away in the recovery process. The sense of disconnection from my usual environment, from the life I knew, was disorienting.

As March faded and April approached, my hospital case worker began to look for a rehabilitation facility where I could continue my recovery. This search was difficult as many facilities closer to Green Bay were fully occupied. The prospect of staying in a rehabilitation center so far from home was daunting. I longed to be closer to familiar surroundings, to reduce the physical and emotional distance that seemed to compound my sense of isolation.

The case worker's efforts were relentless, mirroring the dedication of the entire hospital staff. They understood recovery was about physical healing and emotional well-being, significantly bolstered by proximity to loved ones and familiar environments. The importance of this aspect of care became ever more apparent to me as I faced the possibility of extended rehabilitation far from home.

During this time, the hospital served as a place of healing and a stark reminder of the complexities of medical recovery—challenges that encompass logistical, emotional, and social elements. Each day in the hospital, each visit from Brian, my brother, his wife, my then-wife Beth, and some friends, and each conversation with the case worker were integral parts of recovery, one that extended well beyond the physical injuries I had sustained. I also looked forward to phone calls and texts from my kids, family, friends, and coworkers.

Brian's support and the hospital staff's tireless efforts provided crucial pillars of strength. They helped maintain my spirits, which were tested daily. The care I received went beyond medical treatment; it was a holistic approach that addressed the myriad needs of a person thrown unexpectedly into one of the most challenging situations of his life.

As I looked forward to the following steps, friendship, perseverance, and the profound impact of care—both medical and personal—were ever-present. These continued to resonate with me as I prepared for the next phase of my journey, underscoring this experience's indelible mark on my life.

The days in the hospital stretched into weeks, and each passing moment seemed to linger longer than the last. Yet, within the confines of those walls, I had become part of a community. The staff members, from nurses and doctors to technicians and aides, had become familiar faces—friends, even. Their names and stories were now a part of my daily life, a routine that brought comfort amidst the uncertainty of recovery.

The realization that I was considered a mid-level severity patient ranked about fifth on the scale due to my injuries, was sobering. It put into perspective the gravity of the accidents in our snowy region; others were enduring even greater challenges. This understanding brought with it a sense of camaraderie among us patients. We were all in this fight together, each of us pushing through our battles with the support of the hospital staff.

The attending doctor's revelation also highlighted the extraordinary pressures that the hospital staff faced. They were managing a full house, dealing with cases as severe, if not more severe, than mine. Yet, their dedication never wavered. Each day, they arrived with resolve, ready to tackle whatever challenges lay ahead. Their commitment was professional and deeply personal. They celebrated our small victories and provided comfort during setbacks, making the hospital feel less like an institution and more like a home.

This experience deeply ingrained in me an immense gratitude for the people behind the medical uniforms, for I had known this in my life for many years before this, as Beth was and still is an RN. Their relentless spirit and compassionate approach to care kept me from falling into despair.

In moments of loneliness or pain, there was always a hand to hold and a reassuring voice to tell me that things would improve. They were the unsung heroes who worked tirelessly behind the scenes, ensuring that each patient received the care they needed to heal physically and emotionally.

Chapter 12: Longest 29 Days

After an extensive stay in the hospital, where I'd been to the point where I had become familiar with every hallway and face, the next step in my recovery journey was transitioning to a rehabilitation center. This move was crucial as I could not manage things independently; the simple acts of walking and standing unaided were still beyond my reach.

The physical therapists had only just celebrated the milestone of standing on my right leg for thirty seconds with me, a clear indicator of my current limitations.

The hospital's caseworker became my primary liaison in finding an appropriate facility. Her role was pivotal during this phase as she navigated the challenges of securing a spot in a rehabilitation center during a particularly busy season. Winter in Wisconsin brought snow and ice and a spike in injuries, especially among the elderly, leading to a high demand for rehab services. Most facilities in the Green Bay area were already at capacity, filled with patients recovering from various fractures and surgeries.

After a lot of searching and coordination, my caseworker found a place that could accommodate me. It was situated in Seymour, Wisconsin—a small town about 15 miles from Green Bay. This facility was a combined nursing home and rehabilitation center equipped to handle cases like mine, where extensive physical therapy and care were needed to regain mobility and independence.

The Seymour facility was smaller than the bustling hospital I had grown accustomed to, but it offered a more focused environment tailored to rehabilitation. On my first day there, I was struck by the contrast between the hospital's clinical efficiency and the rehab center's quieter, more intimate setting. Here, the pace was slower, and the approach was more personalized, reflecting the different stages of recovery I was now entering.

Leaving the hospital was a critical turning point in my recovery. Brian, who had steadfastly been there throughout this ordeal, arrived ready to help me transition to the next crucial phase. With braces on both arms and my left leg extended, maneuvering into his car wasn't easy, but Brian managed it with a blend of care and good humor that eased the moment's tension.

The drive to Seymour was quiet, filled mostly with contemplative silence, punctuated by brief exchanges that reflected both the weight of what had passed and the uncertain promise of what lay ahead. I felt relief and apprehension as we approached the Good Shepherd Nursing Home. This facility represented a new beginning, yet another step away from the life I once knew.

Upon arrival, the staff at Good Shepherd were welcoming, quickly attending to me as they unloaded my things. They were gentle and efficient as they transferred me to a wheelchair and took me to my room. This space was to be my new environment for recovery, simpler and quieter than the hospital, but no less important.

My room was functional and plain, and my journey to recovery was far from over. It was equipped with the essentials for someone in my condition, ensuring safety and accessibility. I was alone after Brian left, surrounded by new faces—nurses, therapists, and staff who would soon become familiar through our daily interactions.

During these early days, the solitude was building. While the staff were kind and professional, the absence of family and friends left a void. Brian's visit was a brief respite, a connection to my former life, and his departure marked the beginning of a new, more isolated phase of my recovery.

As I settled into the daily rhythms of the nursing home, my focus shifted primarily to physical therapy—a crucial aspect of my recovery. The routine was rigorous but necessary, designed to rebuild my strength and restore flexibility, which was severely compromised after the ordeal and subsequent surgeries.

The physical therapy sessions were scheduled close to daily, with only Sundays off to rest. Each day, I slowly wheeled myself down the hallway to the therapy room, a place that gradually became a zone of both pain and progress. The routine established by my dedicated physical therapist was methodical and incremental, tailored specifically to my body's abilities and the doctor's instructions on what I could handle, from weight-bearing limits to flexibility exercises.

My therapist, who became a key figure in my recovery, had meticulously planned out a program that began with very basic movements. This included stretching exercises that initially seemed almost trivial in their simplicity. We started with the fundamentals: bending my arms, making fists, and gradually extending these movements to more complex tasks that involved my legs and core.

The simplicity of these initial exercises belied their difficulty. Each movement was a challenge, a battle between my body's limitations and my mind's determination to recover. The pain was constant but dull, and always reminding me of how much I had endured and how far I had to go. Yet, each session brought a sense of accomplishment—to the incremental gains slowly piecing me back together.

During these therapy sessions, my limbs were coaxed back into action, bending and stretching in ways that felt foreign after weeks of immobility. The therapist worked patiently, pushing me to the edge of my capabilities but always mindful of not going too far. The stretches aimed at increasing flexibility were particularly tough. Every small bend and push felt like a monumental effort, but these were critical in preventing the stiffness and atrophy that could impede my recovery.

As the weeks progressed, the intensity of the therapy increased. What began as simple stretches evolved into more complex exercises designed to build muscle strength and improve coordination. The therapist introduced light weights and resistance bands, which seemed inconsequential but proved incredibly effective in strengthening my weakened muscles.

Each day in therapy brought a mix of emotions—frustration at the slow pace of progress, pain from the physical exertion, and, ultimately, a growing sense of hope as I achieved small milestones. The act of making a fist, once taken for granted, now became a symbol of my improving condition. The ability to stretch an arm fully and to bend a knee without feeling excruciating pain were victories in their own right.

The sessions were exhausting, often leaving me drained and sore. Yet, there was an undeniable progression - a slow reclaiming of my body's abilities that filled me with determination. My therapist's encouragement and the visible improvements, no matter how small, motivated me to keep pushing through the discomfort.

This daily physical therapy regimen was a reeducation of my body, learning to move again under the new circumstances of my physical reality. Each session was built on the last, and each day brought me closer to the ultimate goal of walking, perhaps first with crutches and then, hopefully, on my own.

The support of the nursing home staff and the expertise of my physical therapist were invaluable as I continued to navigate this challenging phase of recovery. They guided my physical rehabilitation and also supported my mental and emotional strength, which were essential components of my journey back to health.

As the last week of March rolled into April, I found myself settling into a routine at the nursing home rehab center. Each day began with the hope of making more progress, yet I was constantly reminded of the disparity between my age and that of the other residents. At 55, I was an anomaly here, surrounded by people facing much different, often permanent, life circumstances. This stark reality cast a shadow over my days, making the rehab center feel more confining than it probably was.

Every weekday and most Saturdays, I was pushed to bend, stretch, and strengthen my limbs. The therapy was intense, but it was designed to coax functionality back into muscles and joints that had suffered from prolonged immobility and trauma. Despite the physical strain, the real challenge was mental and emotional. The center was quiet, a stark contrast to the activity of a hospital.

Long and lonely days stretched ahead of me, especially after the structured morning therapies. Afternoons were less about physical recovery and more about mental battles. I would sit in a recliner, working my fingers into clay or squeezing foam pads. Both activities were meant to rebuild my hand strength and also to keep my despair at bay.

The television became my constant companion, filling the room with noise that barely masked the silence of isolation. Occasionally, friends like Brian, my aunt, and cousins would bring snippets of the outside world and reminders of the life waiting for me beyond the rehab center's walls. Yet, when they left, the silence grew even more profound, a reminder of the solitude that had become my new normal.

This solitude was deeply emotional. The reality that many of my fellow residents might never leave the confines of this place weighed heavily on me. It was a daily confrontation with my vulnerabilities and a reminder of the fragility of life. Despite these challenges, the staff's dedication provided much hope. Nurses and therapists tended to my physical wounds and also offered words of encouragement. Their presence was a gentle reminder that recovery was as much about healing the spirit as the body.

The evenings were the hardest. As the rehab center quieted down for the night, the enormity of my situation became more realized. I was left alone with my thoughts, which wandered between the progress I had made and the daunting path that still lay ahead.

These moments, though difficult, forged in me the strength I hadn't known before. They taught me about the depths of my strength and the profound desire to reclaim the life that had been so abruptly interrupted.

As the days turned into weeks, the routine I had once resisted began to offer a sense of stability. Each small victory in therapy, each successful stretch or step, was a building block in the slow reconstruction of my independence. The gratitude I felt toward the staff grew daily; their support was more than just medical care—the empathy and connection sustained me through one of the most challenging times of my life.

The initial solitude began to break with visits from family and friends. About a week into my stay, the faces of my cousins, aunt, and close friends started to appear in my doorway, bringing with them the much-needed comfort of familiar voices and shared memories. Their presence punctuated the monotony and isolation that had settled over me like a thick fog.

The loneliness of those first few days became unbearable. I struggled to sleep, the quiet of the night often pierced by the sounds of other patients in distress down the hall. Television became my companion, filling the silence of the afternoons and evenings until I could surrender myself to sleep. Yet, even with the TV's drone, the nights were long, filled with introspection and a deep sense of loneliness.

The nursing home staff—nurses, doctors, and CNAs—became my lifeline. They did more than attend to my medical needs; they brought human connection into my days. Whether it was helping me shower, bringing meals, or simply checking in on me, their kindness was very powerful during one of the most challenging times of my life. On quiet Sundays, when the activity slowed and the halls became even more silent, their visits to my room were often the highlight of my day.

These staff members were curious about my story. They heard bits and pieces—the man who survived a night in the woods, the miraculous recovery—and wanted to know more.

So, I shared my tale. I spoke of that harrowing night, the desperation, the cold that seemed to seep into my bones, and the unbelievable rescue that brought me to where I was. Each retelling had me relive the trauma, but it was also a therapeutic release, a way to process what had happened.

As I recounted my experiences, I saw horror and fascination in their faces. My survival was not just a medical victory; it had become a story of human endurance. In sharing it, I connected with each listener in a unique way, bridging my world with theirs through the narrative of that fateful night.

With each visit, whether from family, friends, or staff, I felt a little more anchored to the world I had left behind on that snowy night. These interactions reminded me that while my journey through recovery was mine alone, I was not alone in it. The collective support, the shared moments of laughter, and the earnest conversation that was stitched together with communal care enveloped me in warmth and comfort.

In the quiet of the rehab center, every day was a series of small battles and incremental victories. The physical therapy was grueling—far more intense than anything I'd ever experienced, even with my background as a firefighter accustomed to rigorous physical demands. Lying there in the rehab facility, I learned firsthand how challenging it could be to reclaim the simplest bodily functions. The staff's encouragement made the grueling therapy sessions bearable and infused a sense of hope into the recovery routine.

Once strong and agile, my fingers now fumbled clumsily with the pegs on the peg board. The frustration of dropping them repeatedly was demoralizing. However, the therapist was patient, offering encouragement and adjusting the exercises to my slowly improving capabilities. This seemingly simple task became a daily measure of my progress.

The muscle mass I had lost was shocking. The body I had known that carried me through countless fires and rescues now felt foreign and unresponsive. Rebuilding that strength was a painstaking process. The therapy sessions, though essential, left me exhausted and sore. But they also marked small victories in my recovery. Each peg moved, every grip strengthened, signified a step closer to regaining my independence.

During those long days, the loneliness was eating me. I was the youngest person in the facility, surrounded by others who faced many different prospects. Most would likely spend the remainder of their lives in care. This realization was sobering and put my situation into stark relief. It underscored the temporary nature of my stay and fueled my determination to recover and return to my life.

The conversations with staff who tried to uplift me often turned to my ordeal in the woods. Recounting the story became a way to connect with the staff on a personal level. They were fascinated by the details of my survival, and their genuine interest provided a sense of normalcy amid the clinical environment. Sharing my experience also allowed me to process it, to make sense of the trauma and the incredible series of events that led to my being there, lying in a rehab center bed, slowly piecing my life back together.

Through these daily interactions and the relentless physical therapy routine, I began to see tangible improvements. The milestones were small—being able to sit up unaided, standing for more than a few seconds, and taking tentative steps with the support of crutches. Each achievement, no matter how minor it seemed, was a triumph against the odds stacked against me that cold night in the woods.

As I continued to push through the pain and frustration, supported by the dedicated staff around me, I held onto the hope that with each passing day, I was moving closer to recovery. During my time in the hospital and rehab center, the nights often blended into the days, creating a disorienting cycle of sleepless nights and restless days.

On many nights, I found myself wide awake, haunted by vivid dreams and recurring nightmares of lying immobile in the cold, dark snow. These weren't the type of nightmares that jolt you awake, drenched in sweat and gasping for air. They lingered in the back of my mind like a persistent reminder of the trauma I had endured.

During the day, I tried to cling to some semblance of normalcy, following the routine schedule of meals and television that the hospital staff maintained. However, the quiet hours of the night were the hardest. Alone with my thoughts, I couldn't help but think about my future.

Questions raced through my mind: Would I ever work again? Could I live a normal life after such severe injuries? The uncertainty was overwhelming, and the solitude of the nursing home only amplified these feelings.

In the early weeks, especially while I was still wheelchair-bound and dependent on others for basic needs like feeding myself and bathing, I hit what felt like rock bottom. The possibility of not recovering full mobility loomed large, and I struggled to see a clear path forward.

As I lay awake at night, I gradually began to piece together a plan for the future, contemplating how I could adapt and overcome the challenges that were posed by my injuries. The support from the staff and my visitors played a crucial role during this time, offering comfort and distraction from the heavier thoughts that clouded my mind.

As I lay there, each day blurring into the next, the events of February continued to echo loudly in my mind. It was the month everything changed: my separation, the transition of my cabin into my full-time home, and then the crash. Two months later, the weight of those events was truly sinking in. Amidst the physical recovery, I found myself grappling with the mental and emotional toll it was taking.

The isolation was profound. There were days without physical therapy and days I didn't want to face the world. The staff would call to take my meal orders, and sometimes, I'd ask them to shut the blinds so I could escape into sleep, trying to shut out the world. My days and nights became indistinguishable, a disorienting mix of sleep and wakefulness, filled with dreams and half-thoughts I would mull over before drifting off again.

The loneliness was suffocating. During the first few weeks, I was mostly confined to my bed, only occasionally managing to move to a recliner with assistance. Those moments of mobility were brief respites in a sea of inactivity. I found myself repeatedly going over the events of the crash night, trying to piece together every detail, every decision. Did I think that? Did I try this or that? The uncertainty of it all was haunting.

In those endless hours, I struggled not just with physical pain but with the emotional and psychological impact of my situation. The realization of how much my life had changed was overwhelming. It was not just about learning to walk again; it was about learning how to live again, to find meaning and purpose after such a traumatic ordeal. The journey was as much about healing my body as it was soothing my troubled thoughts and finding peace amidst the chaos.

During the long, often solitary days at the nursing home, my television became a lifeline to the outside world, a portal to laughter and normalcy in a setting that often felt anything but normal. Each day, as I tuned into my favorite sitcoms—*Friends, How I Met Your Mother, Seinfeld, and Two and a Half Men*—what seemed like a small routine act took on a greater significance in my recovery process.

With their familiar characters and comedic plots, these shows offered a huge contrast to the nursing home's stark walls and clinical atmosphere. Each episode was a welcome escape, a burst of laughter in the otherwise quiet room. I eagerly awaited the predictable jokes and punchlines, finding comfort in their familiarity. The characters felt like old friends coming over to visit, and their antics were predictable and welcomed distractions from the physical challenges I faced each day.

The power of laughter in healing cannot be understated. Medical studies suggest that laughter can reduce stress, improve pain tolerance, and enhance overall quality of life. In my case, these sitcom marathons weren't just filling time—they were a therapeutic tool aiding in my emotional and psychological recovery. As I laughed at the screen, I could feel the tension in my body ease, the pain momentarily forgotten as endorphins flooded my system.

Moreover, these shows provided a sense of connection to a life I feared had slipped away. The characters dealt with everyday problems, went to work, interacted with neighbors, hung out with friends—normal life events that felt worlds away from the rehab exercises and medical routines I was confined to. This connection was vital. It reminded me that life's regular rhythm was still ongoing, waiting for me once I could join it again.

This unexpected source of comfort also gave me something to look forward to each day. Planning my schedule around the episodes became a ritual. It was a way to structure my day, giving me control over something when so much of my life felt governed by medical appointments and physical limitations. It was a small measure of independence and agency—a way to make decisions for myself.

Conversations with the nursing home staff often revolved around these shows as well. They would pop into my room, check in on me, and linger a bit longer to chat about the latest episode or laugh over a particularly ridiculous sitcom scenario. These interactions, though brief, were deeply meaningful. They broke up the monotony of my days and helped build relationships with the people taking care of me.

As I progressed in my physical recovery, these shows remained a constant companion. Even on days filled with frustration or pain, the predictability of a 30-minute episode—where problems were resolved swiftly and always ended with a laugh—provided a psychological safe haven. My physical isolation was mitigated by the virtual company of characters who had become as familiar as family.

Reflecting on this time, it's clear that the simplicity of watching a TV show became an integral part of my healing journey. The laughter they brought me went beyond mere entertainment; it reminded me of the healing power of joy, the human spirit, and the simple pleasures that sustain us through life's most challenging moments. This experience underscored a vital lesson that small, seemingly insignificant routines sometimes hold the greatest power to heal and comfort us.

I made significant progress through dedication and hard work during my stay at the nursing home. I had regained enough strength and independence to take care of myself, at least to an extent. Then, a day came in late April when I was struggling with a deep depression that had set in, stronger than previous days, and I said to myself, "Rob, you need to leave this place."

While I was happy with my physical progress, my mental progress had stalled. I knew I needed to get back to some normal, whatever that would be. I went to see the facility administrator, whom I had talked to often during my stay and told her I needed to leave. She wholeheartedly agreed. It was time. I would somehow manage on my own from that point.

When I first arrived, I was confined to a wheelchair, barely able to maneuver it with my weakened arms. However, the diligent efforts and care of the rehab team helped me achieve nearly all the recovery goals we had set. Every small step I took in that facility contributed significantly to my recovery, allowing me to reach a point where I could manage most daily activities on my own.

Chapter 13: Homecoming

After significant recovery, my daughter Maddie, alongside her then fiancé Alex, decided to drive from Colorado to Wisconsin to bring me back home. This gesture alone was the love and support that had been my backbone throughout this grueling recovery process.

By Madison's arrival, I had significantly progressed in regaining my mobility. The nursing home had been a place of intense physical and emotional challenges but also of immense growth. I was now using specially ordered platform crutches, which were different from the standard ones most people are familiar with. These crutches supported my forearms instead of just my hands, distributing my weight more effectively and reducing the strain on my wrists. This adaptation was crucial for me, as my arms still lacked full strength, and my hands could not bear any weight.

The day Maddie and Alex pulled up to the nursing home marked a significant turning point in my life. It wasn't just about leaving a facility; it was about reclaiming a part of my life that had been abruptly put on hold.

The drive back to my cabin, now my home, was filled with mixed emotions. On one hand, there was an overwhelming sense of relief and gratitude toward Maddie and Alex for their willingness to help. On the other hand, there was a sense of apprehension about what lay ahead.

As we drove, the familiar landscapes that rolled past the car window brought a surge of memories. Each mile closer to the cabin reminded me of the life I had left behind and the uncertain future I was heading toward. The cabin, which had always been a retreat, was now my full-time residence—a fact that brought both comfort and a reminder of how much my life had changed. The spring season was now upon us, which felt completely different from the world I had known back in February.

Maddie and Alex were incredibly supportive during the drive, filling the car with light conversation and laughter, trying to ease the heavy silence that my thoughts often plunged me into. Their presence was a balm to the lingering fears about my ability to adapt to a life that now had new limits.

Upon arriving at the cabin, the reality of my new situation began to set in. The cabin had always been a place of independence and solitude, which I cherished. However, now it symbolized something different—it was a place where I would have to relearn how to live independently with my new physical limitations.

The transition was daunting. Every step I took with my crutches across the familiar yet now challenging terrain of my home was a step toward reclaiming my independence. Maddie and Alex stayed for seven days, helping me settle in and making small adjustments around the cabin to accommodate my new mobility needs.

Their decision to take time off work to help me settle into my cabin was a gesture that meant more than words can express. During the first few days after my return home, they transformed from family to caregivers, organizers, and chefs, ensuring that everything I could need was within reach.

Their care started with a thorough rearranging of my home. They moved furniture to create clear and accessible paths for my crutches and adjusted the height of essential items so I wouldn't have to reach too high or bend too low. It was about minimizing risks and enhancing comfort, ensuring every corner of my cabin was safe and welcoming.

One of our first stops was the grocery store, where they stocked up on ingredients to prepare meals I could handle on my own once they left. They filled my fridge with homemade dishes like lasagna, soups, and pre-cut fruits and vegetables. These were more than just meals; they were acts of love, prepared to nourish me physically and emotionally.

Maddie and Alex's presence filled the cabin with a warmth that had been missing since my accident. Their laughter and constant chatter turned a space that could have felt like a prison back into a home. Every evening, after the day's chores and adjustments, we would sit together, share meals, and talk about everything and nothing. These moments were a balm to my lonely soul, reminding me of companionship's joy.

Their practical support extended beyond just physical rearrangement and meal preparation. They also helped me schedule ongoing physical therapy at a local clinic, ensuring I could continue my rehab without interruption. This proactive approach was crucial. It provided me with a structure and routine that I would need to maintain my progress.

During those seven days, these two didn't just set up my home; they set me up for success in my recovery journey. They showed me the profound impact of thoughtful, dedicated care. It wasn't just about making my living space accessible or ensuring I had enough to eat; it was about giving me the confidence and means to recover, regain my independence, and adapt to my new limitations.

After they helped me settle in, the real challenge began. It was just me, my cabin, and a long road to recovery ahead. I was still employed at Georgia Pacific, but I knew it would be long before I could return. My body wasn't ready, and my mind was trying to catch up with the harsh reality of my physical limitations.

Living alone with a straight leg brace and not being able to put weight on my left leg presented daily challenges that seemed monumental. This brace meant my leg had to remain extended at all times, turning simple tasks into strategic missions. Imagine navigating stairs, shuffling down hallways, or even getting out of bed with one leg that couldn't bend. Each movement had to be calculated; there was no room for error. If I needed to move, I had to plan each step meticulously to avoid any unnecessary strain or pain.

The inability to bend my leg affected more than just my mobility. It influenced every aspect of my daily life, from personal care to basic household activities. Getting into the shower, preparing a meal, or even getting dressed in the morning became exercises in creativity and patience. I had to adapt to a new way of moving through my world, which often left me exhausted and frustrated. Getting myself in and out of my 4Runner to get to my appointments became a challenge. I'd try to leave early, but I still ended up late!

The solitude of the cabin could be overwhelming. The quiet, once a peaceful solace, now echoed the loneliness of my situation. Without the constant support of family and friends physically there, the days could stretch out endlessly. Yet, this time also forced me to confront my new reality and accept the extent of my injuries. During these quiet moments, I truly understood the impact of what I had gone through and what was still needed to recover.

To keep myself from sinking into further depression, I established a routine that included physical therapy exercises, which I diligently performed multiple times a day. Though painful and exhausting, these exercises were crucial for regaining strength and flexibility. They were not just physical rehab but mental challenges that I had to overcome. Each small movement was a victory, a sign that improvement was possible.

I had to learn to celebrate the tiny triumphs, like the first time I managed to stand alone for more than a few seconds or the first day I could make it through all my exercises without needing to rest every few minutes. These milestones, small as they might seem, were monumental for me. They marked my progress and fueled my determination to return to a semblance of normalcy.

About a week after Maddie and Alex left, I realized that I had to tackle the daunting task of clearing out my place in Colorado. The decision to sell the house where Beth still lived meant packing up a significant chapter of my life. This wasn't about moving physical items but closing a door on a past I had cherished.

Brian, ever the faithful friend, stepped up without hesitation. We planned the trip together—I would handle the finances, like the flight and truck rental, and he would help with the heavy lifting. We were also joined by my good friend Jon, a West Metro Denver Firefighter buddy whose strength would be indispensable given my condition.

I was still navigating life on crutches, making my role in the move more of a supervisor than an active participant. Watching Brian and Jon pack up my belongings into a Ryder truck was bittersweet. Each item, each box, was a memory, a piece of a life that was no longer mine.

Once everything was loaded, Brian, Kelso—my loyal dog—and I set off on the long drive back to Wisconsin. Finally, I was reunited with Kelso. And what a reunion it was. The furry friend I had left in the dark that dreaded night was now back by my side. He was happy, and I was happy. It felt like he forgave me right away, and we were back to being best buds. The journey was a challenge in itself.

Picture this: I'm in the passenger seat, strapped into a straight leg brace that made sitting anything but comfortable, with Kelso squeezed between Brian and me. It was a cramped, occasionally comical arrangement that saw us through an 18-hour drive, complete with an overnight stop to break up the monotony and rest our weary bodies.

The ride was filled with a mix of emotions. There were moments of laughter, especially when Kelso decided he wanted to sit on one of our laps. But there were also stretches of silence, time for me to reflect on my life's changes and the road ahead.

When we finally arrived in Townsend, around the third week of May, I felt a sense of relief. Unloading the truck into my garage, I felt a surge of gratitude for having friends like Brian and Jon. Their willingness to help me through this transition made the physical and emotional load lighter.

With all my belongings in one place, my cabin truly transformed into my home. It was no longer just a retreat from the world but the center of my new reality. Here, I was to rebuild my life, step by tentative step.

This move marked a significant step in my recovery and adjustment to a new normal. It underscored the importance of friendship and support in overcoming life's hurdles. As I settled into my home, surrounded by the familiar from a past life and the tranquility of Townsend, I began to appreciate the full scope of my journey—from the depths of despair in a snowy wilderness to the quiet promise of a peaceful abode. Here, in this space, I could continue to heal, bolstered by the laughter, memories, and the enduring presence of friends and family.

We started unloading the Ryder truck after getting back to Townsend with all my things. Each box and piece of furniture unloaded was like a step further into my new life, into a reality I was still grappling to accept. Brian's help was invaluable, and his presence made the transition smoother. We worked steadily, and by the end of the day, the truck was empty, and my cabin was filled with the tangible memories of my life in Colorado.

After returning the truck, I stood in my cabin, which had now transformed into my home. It was a strange feeling—being back in a place I had always seen as a retreat, a getaway, and now seeing it as my permanent residence. It was comforting yet daunting at the same time. The quiet cabin, surrounded by nature, offered a stark contrast to the bustling life I had left behind. It felt both peaceful and isolating.

I was alone again, but this time it felt different. This time, I was at home. I knew this place would be the cornerstone of my recovery and the foundation for my new life. The first few days of organizing and setting up my space were a blur. I had to create a routine and structure to help me navigate this new chapter.

Cooking became a significant part of my day. It was more than just making meals; it was a way to keep myself busy and ensure I was eating healthily. I started with simple dishes, things I could manage without strain. The kitchen became my little workshop where I would try out new recipes and find joy in the small successes. It was a way to reclaim a part of my independence and remind myself that I could still care for myself.

Every morning, I would make a list of tasks to accomplish. This list kept me focused and gave me a sense of purpose. Whether organizing the garage, doing laundry, or taking a walk with Kelso, these small victories helped rebuild my confidence.

My walks with Kelso became a cherished routine. The fresh air and the companionship of my loyal dog were therapeutic. Though slow and cautious, each step was a testament to my progress.

Physical therapy sessions were a crucial part of my days. Three times a week, I would go to a local therapy center. These sessions were grueling but necessary. The therapists pushed me, sometimes beyond what I thought I could handle. It was painful, both physically and emotionally, but it was also a reminder of how far I had come and how much further I could go. The progress was slow, but each milestone was a beacon of hope, no matter how small.

I often sat in the living room in the afternoons, watching TV. The channel that played all my favorite sitcoms became my go-to, just as in the nursing facility. These shows provided a much-needed escape from the weight of my reality. The laughter and light-heartedness were a balm for my weary soul. They allowed me to forget, even if just for a little while, the struggles and the pain.

But it wasn't all about distraction. I also spent a lot of time reflecting. Nights were the hardest. The silence was deafening, filled with thoughts and memories that would keep me awake. I would lie in bed, thinking about the crash, replaying the events of that night over and over. My mind was trying to piece together a puzzle with missing pieces. Sometimes, the weight of it all felt too much to bear, but I reminded myself of the strength I had shown and the resilience that had brought me this far. For the first time in my life, I truly found out what survival guilt was all about. Or at least I thought that's what it was. I know it's usually defined when someone you love dies, and you are left to deal with it. But in my circumstance, I believe I was going through it at this time. I could not figure out why or how I survived this ordeal. It woke me up at night and sent me reeling, making me think I did not deserve to survive.

During these moments, I often talked to myself, reassuring my scared and uncertain part that everything would be okay. It was a way to soothe my anxiety and keep my spirits up. I knew that my journey was far from over and there would be more challenges ahead, but I also knew I had the strength to face them.

Nick, my son, was a constant presence in my life, even from afar. He called and texted me almost daily from Washington, checking in to see how I was doing and to offer his support. Given the time of the season, he was incredibly busy working at the resort, and coming back to Wisconsin to visit me wasn't feasible. I understood this completely. His work was important, and I didn't want him to feel guilty about not being able to be here in person.

Every call and text from Nick was like a lifeline. Hearing his voice, even through the phone, brought me comfort. It was a reminder that, despite the distance, my family was still close, still connected. We would talk about everything—his work, my recovery, and sometimes just random things to take our minds off the heavy stuff. Nick's sense of humor always shone through, making me laugh even on the tough days.

Maddie and Alex had already done so much to bring me home. Their support during those initial days of my homecoming was invaluable. They organized my house, stocked the fridge, and ensured I was comfortable and had everything I needed. Their presence had been a blessing, soothing the loneliness and helping me adjust to my new normal. Then Brian was always a supporter and a friend who was just a call away.

So, you know, there comes a point in life where the roles between parents and children shift. It's inevitable; as parents age, children often take on the role of caregivers. But for me, this change happened much earlier than I ever expected. I never thought I'd rely on my children for care at this stage. It was humbling, to say the least, to see Maddie and Alex come out and spend those initial seven days taking care of me. They had to help me with everything.

My bond with Maddie grew even stronger during this time. We've always shared a special connection, a similar sense of humor, and a way of looking at life. She's tough and independent, much like I tried to raise her. She's the kind of person who isn't afraid to get her hands dirty, whether changing the oil in her car or figuring out a solution to a problem. Watching her step up and take charge filled me with immense pride. It was a big moment for us that deepened our bond and reinforced our mutual respect for each other.

On the other hand, Nick couldn't be there physically because of his work commitments in Washington. But his constant calls and texts were a lifeline for me. We might only see each other three or four times a year, which is tough, but we make the most of our conversations. Talking to him brought laughter and comfort. We reminisced about old times, shared new stories, and found solace in each other's words. This experience made us realize the importance of staying connected and making time for each other even when life gets busy.

Traumatic events have a way of bringing people closer. They make you pause and appreciate the relationships you have. They remind you of what truly matters. My accident and the subsequent recovery period did just that for my family and me. It made us more determined to stay in touch, visit more often, and cherish our moments together.

The days after my homecoming were filled with small yet significant victories. Every step I took with those platform crutches, every meal I managed to prepare on my own, and every successful physical therapy session was a triumph. It was a slow and often painful process, but knowing my children were cheering me on made all the difference. Their belief in my ability to recover fueled my determination.

In the end, it wasn't just about my physical recovery; it was about the emotional and relational healing that took place. My children became my pillars of strength, and their physical or virtual presence made all the difference. They were my lifeline, my motivation, and my greatest source of comfort. And for that, I will always be grateful.

Chapter 14: Under the Wings

A profound sense of loneliness washed over me when Maddie and Alex left. The cabin, once filled with the comforting sounds of family, now echoed with silence. It was just Kelso and me, facing each day together. The challenges of everyday tasks loomed large, transforming simple routines into monumental efforts. Getting myself in and out of bed at night and in the morning was a struggle. Each movement was calculated, and each step was carefully planned. The absence of Maddie and Alex's support was deeply felt, amplifying the solitude in my home.

Walking was at the top of my list. It was crucial for my recovery, but the process was slow and painful. Even three months after the crash, I was in a straight leg brace until the end of May. The brace constantly reminded me of my limitations, but it was necessary. It kept my leg immobilized, ensuring the bone appropriately healed.

Every day, I had to navigate my home with this rigid constraint, making even the simplest tasks daunting. Getting dressed was a significant challenge. I had to maneuver my shorts over the brace, and every movement required careful planning.

The surgeon emphasized the importance of keeping my leg straight. The bones in my knee needed to heal correctly, and any deviation could compromise my recovery. This meant no bending and no weight-bearing on my injured leg.

The brace stayed on at all times, a constant companion in my journey to recovery. Showering was another ordeal. I had to balance myself on one leg, carefully washing without putting any pressure on my injured limb. The process was exhausting, both physically and mentally.

Navigating my home was a test of endurance. I had a few steps leading into the house, which required careful planning to tackle. If I had a physical therapy appointment, I would start preparing hours in advance. Getting out the door was a major accomplishment. I had to factor in the time it took to get into my 4Runner SUV, a task that was far from simple. Everything took longer, required more effort, and demanded more energy than ever before.

Everyday tasks became my priority. What were once simple routines now required significant effort. Nightly battles were simple actions like standing in front of the sink to brush my teeth, washing up, and trying to get comfortable in bed. I had to arrange pillows under my legs to alleviate the soreness, trying to find a position to allow me to sleep through the night. Mornings were just as challenging. Getting up, moving around, and starting my day were monumental tasks. But I knew I had to push through. I couldn't let the frustration and sadness take over. I had to find a way to maintain a routine, to keep moving forward.

Standing in front of the stove, I could feel the weight of my situation. I was regaining the strength in my right leg, which allowed me to hop around on my crutches. Despite the difficulty, I knew I had to push myself. I couldn't afford to lie in bed or sit in a chair all day. I had to reach deep within myself and find the strength to move forward.

There was no other option.

Driving was yet another challenge. I had to carefully maneuver my crutches into the passenger seat, then hop into the driver's seat, positioning my leg brace as best as possible. The simplest trips to the grocery store turned into hour-long endeavors. Each step, each movement, required careful planning and execution. The things I had taken for granted my entire life now felt like insurmountable obstacles.

The frustration was overwhelming at times. There were moments when I felt my healing was at a standstill. Physically, I was making progress, but it never felt fast enough. The days dragged on, and each was a reminder of the long road ahead. The challenges of getting out of bed, getting dressed, and simply moving around were constant tests of my resilience. It was easy to feel defeated and let the situation's weight crush my spirits.

But I had to keep going. I couldn't afford to sit idle. I had to push myself to do anything to keep moving forward. Whether making a simple breakfast, sitting on the porch to soak up some sunshine, or engaging in physical therapy exercises, I had to stay active. The leg brace and crutches were constant reminders of my limitations but also helped me regain my strength and mobility.

In May, after I settled into my home, I met my brother's friends. Townsend is a pretty tight-knit community, and my brother lived in another community about a half hour away. One day, he mentioned that his friend Todd had just bought a place about a mile and a half from me. I was surprised but excited when my brother told me they were going to come over and visit. It was a chance to meet new people and potentially make some friends in this new environment.

When Todd and his girlfriend Ida came over, they had a new UTV, a utility terrain vehicle, a side-by-side vehicle designed for trail riding. They immediately took me under their wings and formed an instant bond. They mainly were up here on the weekends because they still worked during the week in Green Bay, but I looked forward to those weekends like a kid looks forward to Christmas.

Every Friday, or when I was sore or down, they would come over and say, "Let's go! We're going riding, we're going to have fun, and we're getting you back to a normal life."

As we rode through the trails, the fresh air and the thrill of the ride lifted my spirits. We laughed and joked, and I forgot about my troubles for a few hours. The days they came made me realize how crucial these outings were for my mental health. They weren't just about having fun; they were about healing.

Over time, our bond grew stronger. We celebrated each other's milestones, supported each other through tough times, and built a community that felt more like family. They showed me that even in the darkest times, there are people who care and will go out of their way to make you feel included and valued.

This was a big deal because sitting around the house or on the front porch was so easy, especially given my recent circumstances. Being around them and being active helped me immensely. They made it their mission to include me in everything. Every weekend, without fail, they would take me out in their UTV, getting me out of the house and out of my head.

They have such fun-loving personalities, always ready to enjoy and have a good time. They made it their priority not to let me sit at home day after day.

They lived near Green Bay, which is about 80 miles from Townsend. They would go back home Monday through Wednesday and then return on Thursday or Friday. Each time they came up, they included me in everything—UTV rides, going to eat, barbecues, and other activities. They wouldn't let me sit and feel sorry for myself. Instead, they brought me along on all their adventures, ensuring I was always involved.

Their motive was clear—they wanted to cheer me up and make me feel good. And they did a fantastic job at that. I always felt included; we were constantly joking around and having fun. This helped me not dwell on my issues and injuries or get depressed. At the time, I didn't realize how much it was helping me, but looking back, I see how important it was. I was excited to be doing things and getting away from home.

Eventually, I realized how significant their support was. They included me in everything at their cabin, even when they were remodeling. I helped by supervising and sharing my knowledge on laying ceramic tile and electrical work. Being included in these activities made me feel great, and our friendship continued to grow.

I often reflect on how important this was for my recovery. After getting out of the nursing home, I wasn't sitting at home dwelling on everything that happened. Their insistence on getting me up and out prevented me from falling into a deeper depression. Without them, life would have been very lonely and boring. They played a huge role in my mental and emotional healing, encouraging me to keep going.

We remain good friends, seeing each other at least twice a week. They were a crucial part of my journey, and I am forever grateful for their support and encouragement.

There were times when I felt overwhelmed by my circumstances. The physical pain from my injuries, the emotional toll of being away from my regular life, and the mental strain of adjusting to a new place were all heavy burdens. But Todd, Ida, and their friends provided a much-needed distraction. They gave me a sense of normalcy and belonging that I desperately needed.

Their support extended beyond just the weekends. During the week, we stayed in touch through calls and messages. They updated me on their plans and ensured I was always in the loop. This constant communication made me feel connected and less alone.

Looking back, I realize that their friendship was a lifeline. They helped me navigate one of the most challenging periods of my life. Their support, kindness, and encouragement made all the difference. They reminded me of the importance of community and the power of human connection.

Without them, my recovery would have been much harder. They lifted me out of my gloom, provided companionship, and gave me something to look forward to. They made me realize that I wasn't alone and that there was still joy to be found, even in difficult times.

In the end, it's the people who stand by you during your toughest times who leave the most lasting impact. Todd, Ida, and their friends did that for me when I needed it most.

Reflecting on my journey, one thing becomes clear: I should have sought therapy after leaving the hospital even though I had people who cared for me. Looking back, I realize the importance of mental and emotional therapy. It's a critical part of healing. Some people think therapy is just about going to a professional to be healed, but it's much more than that. It's about having someone to talk to, someone who shows interest in your life and asks the right questions.

Even though my friends and family were incredibly supportive, professional therapy could have provided additional help. During my stay at the nursing home, the CNAs and friends there would talk to me, asking how I felt and whether I needed professional help, like a therapist or psychologist. At that point, I should have taken their advice and sought professional therapy. For anyone reading this story and facing mental or emotional challenges, I urge you to seek the type of therapy that you're comfortable with. If your issues seem beyond your capability, don't hesitate to seek help.

Talking to someone, whether a friend, family member, or a professional, is crucial. Don't hold it in or push it down. You'd be surprised how many people around you might be going through similar issues. Your friends and family will listen to you, and today's world is much more open to discussing mental and emotional health than in the past.

I often think about the time when I was in the nursing home, nearing the end of my stay. Mentally, I couldn't take it anymore. The staff was incredible, but the environment was depressing. I would roam the halls in my wheelchair, seeing the other patients and feeling the weight of the place.

As I mentioned before, I had reached my limit. I went to the director and said, "I need to leave."

She understood and agreed wholeheartedly. She told me to call my daughter. Maddie came two days later, and I left. I knew I still needed a lot of physical therapy, but mentally, I was at my wit's end.

Thanks to the great staff, family, and friends, I made it through that night, the hospital, and the nursing home. But I had to face my thoughts once I was home alone after Maddie and Alex left. There were plenty of channels available for me to seek help. I remembered the Employee Assistance

Program (EAP) from working at the paper mill, which offered access to counselors and therapists. I came very close to using it several times to have someone to talk to about everything I was going through.

I often found myself grappling with survival questions. I kept asking myself why I lived through the ordeal. It was a strange, almost surreal feeling. On one hand, people would say I should be thankful to be alive, but on the other, I couldn't stop wondering why I was spared.

How did I manage to survive lying face down in ten-below-zero weather for twelve hours, with broken bones and all?

It seemed unbelievable to anyone I told.

I was very close to seeking therapy. Then I started spending time with Todd and Ida, and it was a place where people had different mindsets. They didn't allow me to wallow in self-pity. Instead, they helped me see that things weren't as bad as they seemed. Their support helped me begin to move past those dark thoughts and start focusing on healing, both physically and mentally.

They helped shift my perspective. They made me realize that I could get through this and that I would heal, not just physically but mentally and emotionally, too. They were relentless in their positivity, always encouraging me to look at the brighter side of life. This shift in perspective was crucial for my recovery. They kept reminding me that I was lucky to be alive and that there was a reason I survived, even if I couldn't see it at the moment.

Despite this newfound support, the nagging thought of seeking professional help never completely left my mind. I knew deep down that talking to a therapist could help me process the trauma and confusion I felt. But, the constant encouragement and activities with my friends provided a temporary distraction from these thoughts. They kept me busy and engaged, and slowly, I began to feel more like myself again.

However, there were still nights when I lay in bed, unable to sleep, my mind racing with what-ifs and whys. These were the moments when I most felt the absence of professional help. I understood that while my friends and family provided immense support, a therapist could help me delve deeper into my emotions and help me find answers or at least peace with my questions.

Surviving such an ordeal left me with a mix of gratitude and confusion. I couldn't understand why I was still here, but I knew I needed to make the most of this second chance. This internal struggle was something I dealt with daily, even as I tried to move forward. My friends' belief in me and their constant support was invaluable. Still, I also knew that professional therapy could offer insights and coping mechanisms that I couldn't get from friends alone.

I often wonder how things might have been different if I had pursued therapy right away. Would I have found the answers to my questions sooner? Would I have avoided the sleepless nights filled with doubt and confusion? I'll never know. Still, I do believe that therapy would have complemented the support I received from my friends and family, providing a more holistic approach to my healing.

To anyone reading this and dealing with similar feelings, my advice is simple: seek help, whatever form that may take. Friends and family are crucial to recovery but don't underestimate the value of professional therapy. Therapists are trained to help you navigate your emotions, provide tools to cope with your struggles and offer a safe space to explore your feelings without judgment.

In today's world, it's much more acceptable to talk about mental and emotional health. The stigma surrounding these topics is slowly disappearing, making it easier for people to seek the help they need. So, if you're facing challenges, don't wait. Reach out to someone, whether it's a friend, family member, or professional. Talking about your feelings is the first step toward healing.

The emotional and mental healing process is ongoing, and seeking help should be seen as a strength, not a weakness. It's a crucial part of the recovery journey and can significantly affect how you cope and heal.

Now, I remain committed to my mental and emotional well-being. I know that healing isn't a linear process, and it's okay to seek help whenever you need it. My experience has taught me the value of community and the importance of not facing your struggles alone. Help is always available, and reaching out is vital to building a healthier, happier future.

Chapter 15: Rebuilding My Life

As the days of June 2022 unfolded, the weight of physical and emotional recovery began to happen, yet there was a flicker of anticipation each day—a soft, hopeful glow that perhaps today might hold something a little less ordinary. My usual retreats were the local bar and grills near Townsend, just a stone's throw from my quaint home. It was here, amidst the familiar clink of glasses and the comforting aroma of grilled burgers, that life offered me a gentle nudge towards something, or rather someone, transformative.

Sue came into my life during one of these routine outings. With its small-town charm, Townsend was where new faces were noticed and remembered, and Sue's presence was no exception. I was enjoying a casual evening with Todd, my friend who had seen me through the toughest days. Across the room, Sue was engaged in lively conversation with a friend, her laughter a melody that seemed to dance across the bar and weave itself around my senses.

I remember that first interaction clearly. The casual exchange of hellos with her, the way her eyes sparkled with kindness and curiosity when she smiled—a smile that seemed to acknowledge my presence in a world that often felt isolated during those recovery months. Our introduction was simple yet marked by an unspoken recognition as if our souls had, in that brief moment, acknowledged each other's existence in the universe.

In those initial conversations, there was an effortless connection, an understanding that we wove between our words. Each chat we shared by the bar, every laugh that escaped our lips, seemed to stitch my fragmented self a little closer together. I learned her name was Sue, and with one syllable, I felt a warmth that had been absent for too long.

June bled into July, and our encounters grew from coincidental to intentional. We talked about everything and nothing—our favorite books, the best hiking trails around Townsend, and our dreams that seemed a little too audacious to voice until they were shared with someone who believed in them. With her, it felt like rediscovering a part of myself that was lost in the crash—the part that believed in the possibility of new beginnings, of joy that could bloom from the rubble of past pains.

As I strived toward physical recovery, aiming to return to the paper mill that had graciously held my position, Sue became an encouragement. She didn't know all the details of the crash yet, the sleepless nights, the internal battles with doubt and despair, but she saw the strength it took to face each day and cheered on every small victory.

My life began to find a new normal by mid-July, marked by the robust hum of machinery at the paper mill and the soft, anticipatory beats of potential moments with Sue. Returning to work was a milestone—the progress I had made physically and mentally. The familiar setting of the mill, with its towering stacks and the perpetual scent of pulp and sweat, was oddly comforting. Like myself, it was a place of strength, persistently pushing forward despite the past year's trials.

During the same period, my interactions with Sue evolved, weaving through the days like a delicate yet determined vine reaching for sunlight. Each sighting of her had become a highlight of my otherwise structured days. The courage to transform our casual meetings into something more intentional had been simmering within me, and by the second week of July, it boiled over. I asked her out.

The moment was a blend of nerves and excitement, an emotional cocktail that left my heart pounding audibly in my ears. We were at the bar, the same place that had witnessed the tentative beginnings of our friendship. The music was a soft undercurrent to the buzz of conversations, and when I finally voiced my invitation, it was within a split-second decision. I was in the middle of a conversation with Todd when I heard the door close.

I turned around to see Sue and her friend walk into the parking lot. At that point, something deep inside told me to ask her out. I somehow reached the door and out in the parking lot within a few seconds. In time to catch her before they left for the night. I asked her out right there and then. Her response was not immediate; instead, she promised a future encounter, leaving the moment hanging suspended between us, filled with unspoken hopes.

Work became a whirlwind of day and night shifts, making each segment of free time precious. The irregular hours, while exhausting, also heightened my anticipation for each potential meeting with her. The fear of never seeing her again crept into my thoughts during long nights at the mill when the machinery's drone became a canvas for my anxieties.

Then, towards the end of July, a moment of quaint charm unfolded that would etch itself into my memory forever. It was another casual evening that had become the cornerstone of our budding relationship. Amidst light laughter and the clinking of glasses, she placed a piece of paper in my hand—an act so simple yet profoundly intimate in its old-fashioned sincerity. Her phone number was scribbled in a hurried yet distinctly feminine hand. This gesture was refreshingly heartfelt in an age where digital contacts were exchanged with a tap.

Holding the piece of paper, I felt a surge of something beyond the initial sparks of attraction—a deeper connection, tethered by her gesture that spoke of a desire to bridge our worlds outside the spontaneous meetings at the bar. The paper was tangible, a relic of a time when such exchanges held a weight of intention and anticipation.

The quaintness of the act, the deliberate choice to connect through such a personal and tactile medium, struck a chord within me. It was endearing and charming, an echo from a time less complicated by the immediacy of digital communication. Her number in my hand was not just a sequence of digits; it was a promise, a possibility, a whisper of future conversations and shared moments.

This exchange began a new phase, where each call and message would weave us closer, building on the foundation laid by every encounter, every smile, and every shared laughter. As I pocketed the precious piece of paper, I realized that this small, seemingly simple act was monumental in its significance. It was the bridge from casual acquaintance to potential companionship, a leap made tangible by scribbled paper, offering paths to new beginnings and the continuation of our unfolding story.

The gentle sway toward the summer's end brought the eagerly anticipated moment—our first date. By the first week of August, the breezes had softened, carrying the warm scents of late summer, an ideal backdrop for new beginnings.

Sue and I had exchanged numerous texts and calls, leading us to this day when we would meet for pizza—a simple choice but laden with the promise of shared laughter and deeper conversations.

As I approached the pizzeria, a knot of anticipation tightened in my stomach. The tables were adorned with black and white checkered tablecloths, each one a small island awaiting tales of camaraderie and romance. When Sue arrived, the ease with which we greeted each other felt like a relief to the usual awkwardness accompanying first dates. Her smile was just as I remembered, warm and inviting as if it could light up the duskiest of rooms.

As we sat across from each other, sharing a pizza, the conversation flowed as naturally as a river. We delved into each other's stories, peeling back layers with each shared anecdote and revelation. I was struck by how little she knew of my past ordeal, having only heard snippets that barely scratched the surface. She had thought my injuries were the result of something mundane like surgery, not the harrowing night I spent in the woods, a survivor of a crash that nearly claimed my life.

Opening up about that night, explaining the extent of my injuries and the subsequent battle to regain normalcy, felt both vulnerable and cathartic. She listened with an intensity that made me feel seen, her eyes reflecting a spectrum of emotions—from shock to empathy. As she listened, she shared her tales, revealing her essence through stories of triumphs and trials, painting a picture of a resilient and tender woman.

Our bond tightened with each shared story, her presence weaving a tapestry of comfort and motivation around my world. Her vibrant lifestyle, filled with activities like kayaking, walking, and swimming, inspired me. Her vitality was infectious, her spirit bright, and it made me want to be better, to heal not just for myself but to keep up with her, to be part of the world she embraced so fully.

Driven by this motivation, I pushed my physical limits. We started swimming in the lake whenever the day allowed. It was challenging with my injuries, but the cooler water of the lake helped in ways my normal therapy didn't. With Sue by my side, who seemed to be just a few yards ahead, I found a reason to keep pushing. Her patience and encouragement were constant; she never rushed, always waiting with a smile that said she was happy to be together.

The physical exertion was taxing, often leaving me with legs so sore that I could barely feel them. Yet, each time, I was ready for another swim, another chance to be alongside her. The pain was a small price for the joy and sense of accomplishment that came with each outing. With Sue, I wasn't just recovering; I was transforming, finding new strengths, and rediscovering parts of myself that I thought were lost in the crash.

This burgeoning relationship was more than a romantic interest. It was a catalyst for personal growth. Each day spent with her, each conversation, and every small adventure we embarked on together was a step toward regaining my physical strength and rebuilding my inner world, making me whole again, piece by piece. As summer waned, our connection deepened, promising more than just seasonal romance but a partnership that could sustain the changing tides of life.

The more time I spent with her, the more I realized how aligned our journeys were—marked by significant challenges and a relentless commitment to move forward, not just survive but thrive. Our mantra, "keep moving forward," was how our relationship danced. Sue, with her traumatic past, understood the intricacies of healing. Her journey, like mine, was punctuated with moments of pain and resilience, making her not just a partner but a kindred spirit in the truest sense. Our empathy had a profound healing quality as if each shared story and understanding glance were a salve to old wounds.

Each day with her brought new revelations and joys. I found immense comfort in her presence, in the way she listened, really listened, with a depth of understanding that transcended words. Her patience was a gift I had rarely encountered; it was genuine and unwavering. Whether my slow pace during a walk or my need to take frequent breaks during once effortless activities, she accommodated these with a grace that made me feel cherished rather than burdensome.

This patience extended beyond mere accompaniment. When we planned outings, whether a simple visit to a local concert or an adventurous day out, she was meticulous in considering my physical capabilities.

There was no frustration or sighs of inconvenience; instead, there was always a supportive smile and an assuring nod that said, "Take your time. I'm here."

In these moments, I felt the depth of her care, transforming simple acts of patience into love.

Her attentiveness also spilled over into other aspects of my life. She became someone I could rely on for emotional support and practical help. Whether it was an unexpected need around the house or adjusting plans to ensure I could participate comfortably, she was there, ever thoughtful, ever kind.

Each step forward in my recovery was a step towards a future where I could share more and be more with her. I wasn't just motivated by a desire to return to a former state of health but by the desire to participate actively in the adventures I knew we would have.

Her love, a quiet, steadfast force, gave me the strength to push through the toughest days. It was a reminder that healing wasn't just a physical process but an emotional and relational one. Each challenge we faced together, each limitation we turned into an opportunity for growth, strengthened our bond, and deepened our connection. This wasn't just about overcoming adversity but building something beautiful from it, something lasting.

Emotionally, too, Sue was the cornerstone of my stability. Her unending patience and deep empathy for my situation provided a safe space to express my vulnerabilities without fear of judgment. This emotional sanctuary she created was crucial for my mental health, as it allowed me to discuss my fears, frustrations, and hopes openly, something that was vital for my psychological recovery.

Mentally, she stimulated my ambition to heal and keep up with her dynamic lifestyle. Knowing her as an active and vibrant person, I was driven to catch up and be fully capable of sharing in all her adventures. This wasn't about keeping pace physically but about returning to a state where I could engage fully with life and embrace each day with enthusiasm and energy, much like she did.

This drive to match her vitality pushed me into a 'push mode.' It was a mental shift from passive recovery to active pursuit of health. I was no longer content to let recovery take its natural, slow course. Sue's influence imbued me with a sense of urgency—a desire to get better and thrive. Her zest for life was infectious, and it planted in me a deep-seated need to return to normal and reach a new peak of personal well-being.

During these dialogues, I realized Sue and I shared similar childhoods, marked by challenges that forced us to mature too quickly. We connected over tales of independence from a young age—stories that many might shy away from but which drew us closer. This shared past created a bond that was as surprising as it was comforting; I had never before met someone who understood so intrinsically the nuances of a troubled upbringing.

Our conversations often turned to our respective traumatic experiences. I spoke of that harrowing night, lost in the woods, the cold seeping into my bones, the fear. And as I shared, she listened with a depth of understanding that only someone who had faced their darkness could offer. She had her stories of survival, and together, we found solace.

But our bond was not forged in sorrow alone. We found joy and laughter in our mutual love for music, an interest that became a playful and cherished part of our relationship.

We would spend hours listening to classic hits from the '70s and '80s, challenging each other to name the song or artist. These moments were filled with laughter and lighthearted competition, adding layers of joy to our deep emotional connection.

These music sessions, while seemingly simple, were an integral part of our healing process. They allowed us to step back from the heavier aspects of our pasts and enjoy the presence of someone who understood without needing to explain. In these moments of shared happiness, I found my spirit rejuvenating, my mental burdens lifting, and my heart growing stronger.

Another thing we shared was the love of cooking. We would plan and make meals together, not just the ordinary, but try different recipes or make up our own. We even liked the same wines, so we would choose a wine to go with dinner. The meals always tasted better than anything we could have gotten out. But it wasn't just about the food; it was about creating something to enjoy together.

As our relationship evolved, so did our ability to communicate almost telepathically. We grew to understand each other's thoughts and feelings with just a glance or a subtle shift in expression. This deep, intuitive connection was a testament to the strength of our bond, a bond that was both a sanctuary and a source of strength.

Sue was, undoubtedly, the reason I found the courage and motivation to push through the darkest times. Her support was unwavering, her understanding profound. With her, I not only faced my past but began to see a future filled with possibility and hope—a future where healing was not just a distant dream but a present reality.

Chapter 16: Early Retirement

After my accident and subsequent recovery, the rhythm of my career life shifted significantly. By June 2022, I had begun to find a new normal, but the challenges were far from over. Meeting Sue was bright, providing emotional support and a renewed sense of purpose. However, my professional life demanded much of me, adding another layer of complexity to my demanding recovery process.

I was still working at the paper mill in Green Bay, where my shifts were grueling. My work schedule consisted of two 12-hour day shifts, two 12-hour night shifts, and short breaks. Balancing this demanding work schedule with my recovery was no small feat. The physicality of my job at the mill meant that I needed to be in the best shape possible, and yet my body was still healing from the trauma of the accident.

On my days off, I would make the 80-mile trip up to my home in Townsend. This place had become my retreat from the relentless pace of work and recovery. The drive itself, though tiring, was a meditative experience. With Kelso by my side, we would journey, the familiar landscapes offering a sense of continuity and peace.

Arriving at the cabin was like stepping into a different world. The calm, the fresh air, and the beauty of nature were all incredibly healing. It was here that I could take a breath, slow down, and focus on my therapy without the distractions of work. The cabin wasn't just a physical space but a mental and emotional refuge.

The days I worked were particularly challenging. The shifts were long and demanding, leaving little time for anything else. I would finish at 6 p.m. on day shifts, quickly shower, and then drive up to Townsend. Night shifts were even more grueling. I would come home in the morning, grab breakfast, and then sleep for a few hours before returning to work. These days blurred together, a cycle of work and sleep with little room for anything else.

However, the pain from my injured knee seared through me like a relentless storm, marking every shift at the mill with a stark reminder of my physical limitations.

Each workday was a gauntlet that began with a detailed trek across the expansive parking lot. This walk, while only a 10 to 15-minute journey, felt like a 20-mile hike, each step sending sharp reminders of the trauma my body had endured. As I maneuvered through the seemingly endless asphalt, I focused on warming up my muscles, which had atrophied from weeks of inactivity. This routine, intended to prepare me for the day, was my daily battle against my body's rebellion.

The work environment, with its industrial demands, was less than forgiving. Stairs had to be climbed, and distances traversed within the sprawling mill to reach my workstation. Initially, the movement helped keep the stiffness at bay. However, as hours ticked by, a deep ache would set into my bones, gnawing at my resolve. The occasional chance to sit brought no relief. Contrarily, it was a trap; each attempt to rise after resting was a battle against stiff, protesting muscles, leaving me worse off than before. I learned quickly that mobility, however painful, was preferable to the agony of reawakening my limbs after stillness.

The seasonal transition into the late summer months did little to ease my discomfort. My job often required me to kneel or crouch, maneuvers that seemed simple yet were Herculean tasks for me. Machinery maintenance, a routine task, became a significant hurdle. The need to kneel and address issues like paper jams under conveyors or adjustments that couldn't be made from standing became dreaded tasks.

I remember vividly the panic that set in the first few times I found myself unable to rise from the ground. Alone, without immediate help, I struggled to find leverage, reaching out for anything within grasp—a handle, a bar—to pull myself up. The fear was real, a mix of frustration and vulnerability, as my legs refused to cooperate, locked in a painful rigidity that no amount of willpower could overcome.

Kneeling pads scattered around the tool storage areas became my aid and my adversary. They offered a cushion against the hard factory floor but mocked my attempts to rise without assistance. The pressure on my knees was immense, the scar tissue binding my movements as effectively as any physical restraint. Each session of physical therapy was a battle against this internal scarring, a painful process of breaking down barriers that my body had hastily erected in the wake of the crash.

Despite diligent efforts in therapy, progress was painfully slow. Flexibility exercises, designed to restore movement, felt like a cruel test of endurance. The scar tissue was stubborn, an enemy that refused to yield quickly. Each stretching exercise was a mix of hope and despair, a battle between the desire to heal and the raw, physical reality of my condition.

My job at the mill was physically taxing, even under normal circumstances. I operated a machine that produced trifold paper towels. This job required constant vigilance and quick reflexes to keep the machine running smoothly. The work was fast-paced, and I had to frequently switch parent rolls, fix paper jams, and manage any other issues that arose. The physical demands were relentless. I was on my feet for most of my 12-hour shifts, covering significant distances as I moved around the machine, making adjustments and ensuring everything ran efficiently.

Each shift felt like a marathon. The repetitive motions and the need to stay alert were exhausting. My body, still healing, struggled to keep up with the demands. My strength was not what it used to be, and my flexibility was severely limited. By the end of each shift, my entire body ached. The pain in my legs and arms was a constant reminder of my injuries, and I often found myself battling fatigue as I tried to stay on top of my duties.

The nights were tough. After a long night shift, I would be completely drained. I had to push through the exhaustion to drive back to Townsend. Leaving the mill at around 6:30 in the morning, I often fought to stay awake during the 80-mile drive. The journey was a test of my endurance and willpower. Arriving at my cabin, I would collapse into bed, desperate for sleep but wary of wasting my precious days off recuperating entirely.

Sleep, when it came, was fitful. The pain in my body made it difficult to find a comfortable position. I would toss and turn to ease my legs and arms discomfort. Getting up in the morning was a struggle. The simple act of getting out of bed required a careful, deliberate effort. This routine was taxing and often left me feeling frustrated and disheartened.

The mental toll of these challenges was significant. The constant pain and effort required to perform even the simplest tasks affected my spirit. There were days when I felt overwhelmed by the sheer difficulty of it all. The isolation at my cabin, while peaceful, also contributed to a sense of loneliness. I missed the easy companionship of my family and friends, the simple joys of spontaneous visits and shared meals.

Despite the hardships, there were moments of respite. Spending time with Kelso, my loyal companion, and sharing time off with Sue provided a much-needed distraction from the pain. These times were comforting, a reminder that I was not completely alone. We would sit together on the porch, enjoying the fresh air and the quiet of the forest. These moments were small but significant, offering a brief escape from the relentless demands of my recovery.

In those sweltering summer months, as the mill's interior mercilessly climbed to a blistering 100 degrees, my daily reality was a brutal symphony of heat, pain, and relentless physical demand. Each day was a battle, not just against my injuries but against the oppressive heat that suffocated any relief I might have found. As the temperatures soared, so did my discomfort; the air was thick and heavy, laden with the relentless buzz of machinery and the stifling heat radiating from every surface.

Extra strength Tylenol became my constant companion, a necessary ally against the relentless pain. I always kept a large bottle in my backpack, a routine that became as habitual as clocking in for my shifts. With each pill, I hoped to stave off the worst of the pain, to keep my body functional enough to endure yet another day on the factory floor. Hydration was another battle.

The mill ensured each workstation was stocked with a pallet of water cases, recognizing the critical need to keep workers hydrated in such extreme conditions. My coworkers and I would often go through a case and a half each shift, the constant water intake a testament to the draining environment we were forced to endure.

This regimen—Tylenol and water—was punctuated by strategic eating, small bites throughout the shift rather than full meals that could weigh me down. This approach helped manage my energy levels, but the physical exertion was still a colossal challenge. Walking, the simplest task now marred by my injuries, was a massive effort. Each step was laden with pain, each movement a reminder of the accident that had so drastically altered my life.

After each grueling shift, I returned to my duplex that I had rented when starting my job at the mill. I did this to be closer, so I wouldn't have driven back and forth to Townsend daily. Here, I would engage in the essential routine of icing my knees and the elbow I had broken. The cold was a harsh but necessary contrast to the day's heat, a temporary relief from the constant ache that enveloped my joints. These sessions, while painful, were crucial, helping to reduce inflammation and provide a measure of relief that was my only respite.

As the year wore on and the leaves shifted from vibrant greens to the muted hues of autumn, my resolve began to falter under relentless pain and physical limitation. By mid to late November, a profound weariness had settled in my bones. The daily exertion at the mill—a job I once performed with vigor and passion—had become a grim reminder of the restrictions my injuries imposed on me. The reality was stark: despite my determination, I was not healing. If anything, I was regressing, my body losing the battle against the demands I continued to place on it.

The mill required extensive physical activity; it was not uncommon for workers to clock in over five miles daily, a statistic proudly tracked by apps and shared among coworkers. This was a testament to the job's intensity for a fit individual. For me, it was a near-impossible feat. With my muscle mass significantly reduced, likely around 40% of what it once was, each step was a laborious effort, each task a mountain to climb. The physical toll was matched only by the mental strain of knowing I was far from my best self.

As my proficiency with the machinery increased, thanks to a comprehensive training program, so did the realization that full independence in the role would only exacerbate my physical issues. The more I learned, the clearer it became that I could not meet the job's physical requirements nor perform to the standards I held for myself. This realization was a heavy blow to my professional identity and sense of self.

By December, the internal dialogue that had been a murmur of doubts became a clear, undeniable voice: I needed to change my path. The winter brought its challenges, the cold seeping into my already aching bones, making outdoor activities on my days off unfeasible and further isolating me. During this time of reflection and stark realization, I decided to step down from my role at the mill.

To their credit, Georgia-Pacific had been accommodating, attempting to find a position within the company that would be less taxing on my body. They offered various roles, but each involved prolonged periods of standing or walking—activities that were now my nemesis. Despite their best efforts and my desire to continue, it became evident that the physical demands of almost any job there were beyond what I could handle.

The decision to retire was not made lightly. It came with a deep sense of loss—for the job I loved, my colleagues, and a part of my identity tied deeply to my work ethic and professional capabilities. My co-workers at the mill had become like a second family. Their youthful energy and shared commitment to the job had been a source of joy and inspiration. Georgia-Pacific was more than just a workplace; it was a community where I had felt valued and supported, with excellent benefits and a strong corporate culture that made the daily challenges somewhat bearable.

However, as the year closed, I had to accept that continuing in this environment was untenable. It was not just a physical surrender but a mental one. Once a source of pride and fulfillment, the work reminded me of my limitations. This realization brought a profound sadness, a mourning for the career I loved and the future I had envisioned within the industry.

The history of papermaking, which had captivated me, the machines I had operated, and the process I had been a part of, were now parts of a life I had to leave behind. My passion for the industry, the art and science behind each product we created, was still strong, but my body could no longer comply with the demands.

As I stepped back from my role, I resolved to focus on my health to reclaim some semblance of normalcy in my life. This next chapter, while uncertain, was necessary. It was a step back to hopefully move forward, to heal, and perhaps find a new path that accommodated my new realities. This was not just an end but a beginning—albeit a reluctant one—of a journey to redefine my capabilities and rediscover my strengths in a new context.

Transitioning from the relentless pace of mill life to the tranquil surroundings of Townsend marked a shift in my journey. In December, as I finally settled into what would become my permanent residence, the contrast between the industrial din of my previous life and the serene silence of the snow-covered landscapes was seen and felt. It was here, amidst the towering pines and the quiet hush of winter, that I focused intently on my rehabilitation.

The first order of business was to reclaim my physical health, which had deteriorated significantly. The duplex, which had served as a temporary anchor during the tumultuous months of work, was no longer needed. Cleaning it out felt symbolic, like shedding a layer of my past that was cloaked in pain and struggle. Sue helped me move what was left to move, and then it was done. Another chapter was completed. Once settled in Townsend, the real work began—focusing on flexibility and regaining the strength in my legs that had been sapped by injury and overexertion.

Snowshoeing with Sue became my therapy, both physical and mental. The abundant snowfall that year provided the perfect low-impact exercise. Trudging through the thick, forgiving layers of snow, each step was a gentle challenge to my muscles and joints, a far cry from the harsh, unyielding factory floor. The resistance of the snow provided the necessary workout to build strength without the painful impact of harder surfaces. It was an exercise in patience and gradual progress, learning to listen to my body's needs and pushing it just enough to gain strength without causing distress.

The daily routine of venturing onto the frozen lake, sometimes for an hour or two, became a meditative practice. The crisp air filled my lungs, invigorating and chilling all at once. The rhythmic crunch of snow under our snowshoes was a soothing soundtrack to my thoughts, which wandered as freely as my path across the ice.

On warmer days, I would strip down to a T-shirt, feeling the paradox of sweat cooling on my skin in the freezing air, a testament to the effort exerted in the peaceful solitude.

This new routine brought a gradual but noticeable improvement. The rest periods between my snowshoeing expeditions allowed my body to recover and strengthen. It wasn't just the physical act of moving through the snow that healed me, but the rhythm of activity followed by rest, mirroring the natural ebb and flow that I had denied myself during the relentless work schedule at the mill.

As the weeks turned into months, we ventured into other activities. Simple walks down the road, the distance gradually increasing as my legs grew stronger. Small projects around the house or short drives into the countryside kept me busy, each task a step towards normalcy. The routine I established was therapeutic, a balanced mix of exertion and relaxation that nurtured both body and spirit.

The solitude of Townsend was quite different than the bustling mill. I missed the laughter and shared purpose with my colleagues, yet I found a new kind of companionship in the quiet of the woods and the occasional wildlife I encountered. The emotional journey was as significant as the physical, with moments of reflection interspersed with growing contentment and hope.

Chapter 17: Change in Perspective

For the most part, feeling like I was so close to the end of my life at such an early age made me stop and reflect. It was like I finally had my moment to stop and smell the roses. Before this, my life was always in a rush. I was preoccupied with my work and my home life, and I was constantly putting things off or procrastinating.

This experience gave me a new perspective on things. Now, I don't sweat the little things. I focus on the people around me, the ones I hold dear—my kids, friends, and relatives. My outlook on life has changed incredibly in this way.

It was truly my "stop and smell the roses" moment. I had been taking things and people for granted, believing I could do the tasks I put off the following day or the next. I learned to value the things that were important to me and the things that I wanted to accomplish, like traveling and seeing old friends and family.

You know when you say, "Oh, we should get together," but it never happens. Now, I make it a point to follow through and not let years go by without seeing the people I care about. My perspective on life has shifted significantly. Now, I prioritize the important things and let go of the unimportant ones—the things that slow me down or clog my mind. The useless drama, the gossip, people talking about other people. I stay away from it. My new outlook still holds for me today, and I'm happy.

Over the years, my friend Brian, from the fire department, has tremendously supported me. We remain really good friends to this day. He helped me in countless ways, especially during my move and getting my place set up here. He was there for everything. Brian visited me often, kept my spirits up, and made me laugh—a significant boost during tough times.

My Aunt Dar has also been a constant presence in my life. She messaged, called, and visited me while I was in the nursing home, and she kept on being there for me. She genuinely wanted to be a part of my life and help in any capacity she could. My cousin, Lisa, with her ever-present smile, made an effort to meet me for lunch and kept me laughing and moving forward.

Then there are my friends, Todd and Ida. They encouraged me and helped me day by day. They are a major part of my life, and I see them twice or thrice weekly. They're always there for me with laughter and fun activities, and they provide emotional support, which has been crucial for my mental and emotional well-being.

My kids, Nick and Maddie, and my son-in-law, Alex, have also been huge sources of support. Despite the distance—two in Colorado and another in Washington state—they're always just a text or call away. They provide laughter, support, and a sense of connection, even if we can't be together often.

Of course, my girlfriend, Sue, has been an incredible source of help and motivation. She has continuously encouraged me to progress and supported me in reaching my physical and emotional goals. We travel often, visiting our blended family of four adult children. She has two incredible daughters, Amanda and Kailyn, who have become a big part of my life completing my extended family. We always look forward to spending time with all of them. We are starting new traditions and making new memories.

The friends I've made in the small community of Townsend have also been uplifting, and they are always ready to have a good time, whether going out for a meal or sitting around the campfire. They are quick to lend a hand with a project or lend an ear to listen. We share the same humor and love to laugh, which makes me look forward to our time together.

All these people have played significant roles in my recovery and daily life. They've helped me through conversations about my experiences, nightmares, and how I'm coping. Their support has been invaluable.

As for how I value life now compared to before the incident, it's challenging to explain unless you've been at that threshold. When you're on the brink of giving up all hope, you're at the end and somehow survive; it changes you. People often ask me how I made it through that night, and honestly, I don't understand it. It feels like a dream at times.

Before this incident, my life was in a world of change. I was searching for my self-worth, my purpose. Now, I feel the values of my life have shifted. The incident and the people who helped me—from the night it happened to my recovery in the hospital and nursing home—put a huge value on my life. It made me realize the importance of staying positive and appreciating every moment.

It's unfortunate that sometimes, it takes such an incident for us to understand the value of our lives truly. Now, I see every day as a gift, and I'm grateful to wake up and sleep with a sense of happiness. Of course, there are bad days, but I still view this as my second chance. For reasons I can't explain, I should have died that night, but I didn't. That realization has given me a new outlook on life.

It's a powerful reminder that everyone's life has value. Life is precious, whether at rock bottom or the top of your game. You only get one shot, and I intend to make the most of mine in the years ahead.

For years, I challenged myself in everything—BMX and motocross racing, firefighting, you name it. I never gave accidents or injuries any attention; they just felt like a part of the excitement. I never gave close calls a second thought, whether I was on a Harley or a sled or in a fire. I thought I was unbreakable, a living, breathing suit of armor.

I continued moving ahead despite fractured bones and other wounds because the adrenaline kept me going, and I refused to accept my limitations. That was a grave error. I've understood that the human body functions more like a high-performance engine that needs regular maintenance. I need to slow down and start looking after myself more. I should value and respect my body, mind, and soul since I'm not invincible. It's time that I stop taking needless risks and start treating myself with the same respect and care that I gave to those who I've helped from their accidents and injuries.

I look at the world differently now. It is no longer about taking risks or avoiding peril. It's about learning to love the amazing machine that keeps me going through life. My body is my vehicle through life that requires respect and care, not merely a tool for testing boundaries. And it goes beyond. I became aware of the toll on my mind and emotions that I didn't realize were there—stress, lack of sleep, and being on high alert all piling up.

It is about accepting a different power rather than focusing on one's limits. It's the ability to prioritize taking care of oneself, slow down, and enjoy being in the present. It's about hearing what my body is whispering before it yells. Real bravery is realizing that life is fragile and treating oneself with the same kindness that one shows to others.

After nearly losing everything, I have come to value friendship much more. I am deeply grateful for the support of my friends during my toughest moments. When I was at my lowest, those that checked in with me showed that they cared and asked how I was doing or if I wanted to talk truly stood out. Regretfully, there are times when a major event requires you to completely understand the significance of the individuals in your life who genuinely love you and are prepared to help you through your daily challenges and recovery process.

Due to this event, I now focus on only a few close friends. I've never been good at communicating, which even got in the way of my previous relationships. These days, I try to stay in contact with my friends and value our time together. These friends have become an integral part of my life, and they have given me happiness, encouragement, and a feeling of community.

This event completely changed my outlook on life and caused me to appreciate every day more. My priorities have shifted dramatically, and now I focus mainly on my well-being and mental health. After retiring, I concentrate on looking after myself as a whole: physically, emotionally, and mentally. In this regard, I set small, achievable objectives like going for walks, working out, or participating in daily activities that bring happiness into my life. This has helped me enjoy simple things in life or get satisfaction from such little things.

I have found better fulfillment and happiness in the level of quality daily experiences and the depth of relationships. This has been life-changing—such intentional living helped me recover and thrive beyond anything conceivable before this event.

We all have the honor of being a part of this precious gift called life, and when we have come close to losing it, we are grateful for this knowledge of life a lot more than before. My time after the event has offered me a fresh viewpoint that I never had before, and the aims I have set for the moment are an outcome.

I now place greater emphasis on the subjective aspect of my life, understanding that no one can guarantee they still have time to live. I would never have thought that surviving this crash would practically ensure I had more time to live, and thus, I intend to make the most of my time. My aims are mainly how to improve my existence, i.e., I plan to travel, take care of my close relationships, and manifest more love and courtesy to my friends and family. I try to avoid those who waste time in drama and lose focus on what is essential.

Many people allow drama to dominate their thoughts and actions, whether related to politics, religion, or personal conflicts. I have made it a goal to stay open-minded and focus on my life without getting dragged into such negativity. This approach includes setting mental and emotional goals, such as maintaining a positive outlook and avoiding unnecessary conflicts.

Physically, I am still on the path to recovery. The crash significantly impacted my flexibility, endurance, and overall physical health. For the first year, even simple tasks left me feeling exhausted. However, I am now in a better physical state, and in many ways, I am in better shape than before the crash, except for some lingering issues with my legs and knees. My goal is to continue improving my physical condition and regaining the endurance I once had. I want to reach a point where I can run up several flights of stairs without feeling winded.

Sue has been instrumental in my physical recovery. We motivate each other to stay active and push our limits. Just today, we went swimming, pushing ourselves to swim further than we thought possible. Although I am sore now, it's a reminder of my commitment to physical fitness. I am approaching my 57th birthday and refuse to feel like I am much older. My goal is to feel youthful and energetic.

Another crucial goal is to treat my friends and family with the respect and love they deserve. They have stood by me through thick and thin, and it is important to show my appreciation. I also want to travel and set achievable goals, ensuring that I accomplish them. Sue and I have been traveling throughout the United States, visiting our kids, and we have talked about one day going to Europe. So far, I am making good progress in this area.

In summary, my experience has led me to prioritize the quality of my life. I am creating a fulfilling and enjoyable life by setting meaningful goals, maintaining strong relationships, staying physically active, and avoiding unnecessary drama. All of this may sound cliché, but I know now first-hand what it's like to be incredibly close to the end, and it truly makes me realize how important these things are.

Chapter 18: Gratitude

When someone hits rock bottom, they are more likely to listen more closely to their friends and family. You start to realize you are dependent on them at this time in your life. Although you don't want to bother them, you must understand that you can't function emotionally and mentally without their assistance. Everyone goes through terrible moments, whether a small setback or a major catastrophe. In these moments, you must realize the actual worth of your connections.

I found that small gestures from others made a huge difference, even when I was at my lowest. A simple text message or a quick hello meant the world to me. When I was in the hospital, I was unable to use my hands. At that time, the nursing staff and CNAs helped me by reading my texts and responding on my behalf. Although this would seem small, these acts of kindness were crucial during my recovery.

It might be difficult to depend on people and be vulnerable, yet doing so is frequently the only route through difficult situations. In the process, you understand the importance of your friends, family, caretakers, and relatives. And for those who find it hard to trust – all I have to say is that you have to breathe deeply, surrender to their care, and have faith in their ability to assist you. Having someone to talk to made the healing process a little easier, and despite my fears, I had to remind myself that I was in excellent hands constantly.

Every interaction, no matter how brief, brought me closer to recovery. Even if it was just for half an hour or an hour, those moments of connection were necessary. Whether they knew it at the time or were just being nice, courteous, or caring, after every text, phone call, or visit, I felt emotionally drained. I appreciated their presence; it briefly took my mind off things. I'd feel uplifted, and then when they had to leave, returning to their own lives, I'd hit a low.

I looked forward to their return, cherishing their daily messages. Despite their busy lives with work, family, and friends, I never took their support for granted. I hope others realize the incredible impact our friends, family, and acquaintances can have on us in critical moments, often without realizing it.

One instance stands out regarding the hospital and nursing home staff, who played a significant role in my recovery. Let me start with the rescuers, hospital, and nursing home staff.

Firstly, my deepest gratitude goes to Ron, my hero, who intervened and set everything in motion—the rescue, hospital care, and recovery. Without him, I can honestly say I wouldn't be here today. Our conversations revealed he was as affected by the incident as I was. His decision to turn back on that trail and noticing a glove was nothing short of fate. I can't express enough how thankful I am to him.

Similarly, the rescuers, EMTs, and flight nurses who found me in the woods with two broken arms and legs on a freezing morning deserve immense praise. They packaged me up despite the bitter cold, working tirelessly to get me to safety. Their selflessness in such extreme conditions leaves me speechless. Having been on the other side for many years, responding to emergencies in all weather, I know firsthand the dedication required—they deserve recognition, even though they never seek it.

The rescue and recovery was a coordinated team effort from Ron to the nursing home staff. Upon arrival at the hospital, the trauma team, including the helicopter crew, nurses, and doctors, prevented me from slipping into shock—both mental and emotional. They reassured me and communicated that they were doing everything possible, avoiding the false optimism that can be common in their field. They emphasized providing the best care available, which was crucial as I remained in critical condition. Their thorough assessment and careful handling were flawless, even as I joked about my numbness.

Expressing gratitude remains paramount, as I intend to thank each individual involved personally. Their dedication contrasts with routine emergency calls, where severe cases like mine are less frequent but significantly impactful. The hospital staff at Aspirus Hospital in Wausau acted swiftly and decisively, displaying exceptional teamwork throughout my initial month of treatment. Whether boosting morale or performing necessary procedures with care, their presence made a profound difference during those critical moments.

Their compassion and human touch, from reassuring words to sharing meals during breaks, made my hospital stay more bearable. Their commitment to teamwork and genuine care resonates deeply, underscoring the importance of their roles in my recovery journey.

Feeling better was immediate, just through human contact and emotion. The staff at Aspirus would come in and, knowing I was something of a mini-celebrity, ask to eat lunch or chat with me during breaks. These moments were crucial in my healing process, offering comfort and distracting me from pain. They were incredible. Never did I feel alone or scared in their care. They fed me, cleaned me up, and made me as comfortable as possible. Always with no complaint or comment. Each small interaction, whether a conversation or watching a show together, reassured me that my recovery was possible.

Transitioning to the nursing home, I initially felt like I should prioritize others' needs over mine. Instead, they insisted I needed care and support, too, and encouraged me to lean on them. This care continued through my four weeks there, where I received constant attention and kindness despite their usual older clientele. They were quick with a story or just conversation about their normal lives. This distraction from my current life then really helped me to calm my inner self and to realize things are going to be alright.

Returning to Townsend was like coming home, albeit quietly. At the grocery store or local bar, friends wanted to hear my full story, not just bits and pieces. Their warm reception and willingness to assist—holding doors and helping with errands—meant a lot. As I integrated back into the community, many knew my story and expressed relief and support for my recovery.

People's reactions, from discussing my ordeal to recognizing me as "that guy," amused me. It became a talking point in town, where everyone seemed to know about someone who survived a harrowing experience in the woods. Their curiosity and genuine concern made me feel welcomed and appreciated as I regained normalcy.

And then they would come up to me, noticing my crutches and leg brace, and ask what happened. As soon as I told my story, they'd exclaim, "Oh, you're that guy!" It happened so often that I jokingly considered naming this book "Yes, I'm That Guy." My friends and everyone started calling me "That Guy," which I found amusing. Sometimes, I'd beat them to it and say, "Yep, I'm that guy," before they could.

Also, I was alone and not looking for a partner at the time. I was focused on recovering and finding my new normal. I first noticed Sue at the Sunset Resort, a local bar. I had seen her around before; she had this smile that lit up the room, and she was always friendly and quick to say hello. After a few conversations, I found myself thinking about her constantly. She seemed to brighten my day without even trying.

Once we started going out, I realized she was someone special.

I believe in "If it's meant to be, it'll be," and meeting her felt like fate. She came into my life for a reason: to support and inspire me to recover and set new goals for myself and our future together. She was crucial to my mental, physical, and emotional recovery, making me want to be better every day.

She had a traumatic past, and so did I. We were both searching for something similar - a reason to keep going. It wasn't about forgetting the bad times or moving on but about moving forward and finding happiness together. We craved a partnership, and that's exactly what we found in each other at that point in our lives. It just clicked. We came into each other's lives for a reason, and from that moment on, we've kept moving forward.

We were active together. We swam, worked out, walked, biked, kayaked - constantly pushing each other physically. But even more importantly, those first few months were crucial mentally and emotionally. We had deep conversations about our feelings, our mental state, and how we could support each other and grow. Keeping those conversations open was the key. There were tough days, for sure, but they were far outnumbered by the countless happy ones.

Through these conversations, we learned a lot about ourselves and each other. We rebuilt our mental resilience and found incredible value in our partnership. Being in a healthy relationship again was a major step forward for both of us.

After my mom passed away from COVID in December 2020, my Aunt Dar became the matriarch of our family as my mom's last living sibling. She stepped up immediately. Previously, she lived near my duplex in Green Bay, so I often helped her with things around the house on my off days or after work. This brought us closer. We used to be close during my childhood, attending birthday parties and family events. Over time, like many families, we drifted apart, but reconnecting during this period was significant. Helping her with practical tasks around her house strengthened our bond.

She is an amazing woman. She reached out as soon as she learned of my accident and hospitalization, sending me texts and phone calls that demonstrated her unshakable support. It seemed like having a little piece of home nearby during such a trying period, and having her support was reassuring. She was a big part of my recovery and came to see me at the nursing home with my cousin Lisa and even brought me snacks to cheer me up.

The reconnection with most people I once knew struck a powerful chord. It served as a stark reminder of how precariously close I came to losing everything. It felt like a miracle or something very close to it. The outpouring of support and care from family and friends during my recovery washed over me. They were attentive listeners, asking thoughtful questions, and genuinely invested in my experience and well-being.

Reconnecting with loved ones, particularly my cousin Lisa, was special. Despite facing her tragic experiences years ago, Lisa has always exuded an infectious zest for life, embracing each moment with vibrancy. As I reclaim my life and make the most of this second chance, her spirit is an inspiration I aim to embody.

The gift of renewed time has ignited a burning desire– to cherish every moment with loved ones and forge deeper connections. I want them to understand the immense depth of my love, appreciation, and devotion. I will stand by them, unwavering, through any challenge.

Life has a way of coming full circle, presenting us with hurdles and moments of need. The firm support we offer one another, without judgment or hesitation, has become a value I hold most dear. In our darkest times, this support becomes our lifeline.

Writing this book has helped me move forward mentally and emotionally. While I still, to this day, wonder how and why I made it through that night, I tell myself it's because I have more living to do. As this chapter in the "story of my life" comes to an end, I look forward to seeing what the rest of my chapters bring.

www.ingramcontent.com/pod-product-compliance
Lightning Source LLC
Chambersburg PA
CBHW070717160726
47998CB00023BA/320